1/04

Native Healing

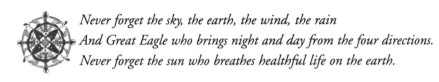

Never forget the sky, the earth, the wind, the rain
And Great Eagle who brings night and day from the four directions.
Never forget the sun who breathes healthful life on the earth.

– Song of the Plains People

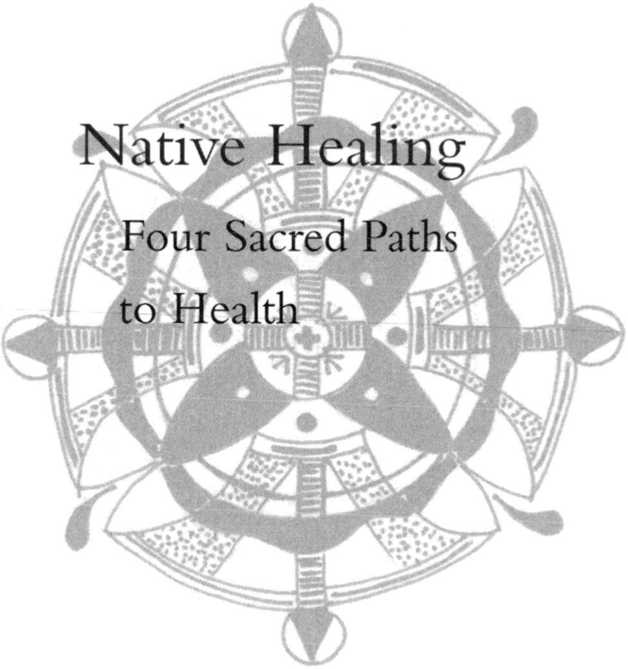

Native Healing

Four Sacred Paths to Health

W.F. Peate, M.D., M.P.H.

Rio Nuevo Publishers
Tucson, Arizona

Rio Nuevo Publishers
An imprint of Treasure Chest Books
P.O. Box 5250
Tucson, Arizona 85703-0250
(520) 623-9558

Library of Congress Cataloging-in-Publication Data
Peate, Wayne F.
Native healing : four sacred paths to health / by W.F. Peate.
p. cm.
Includes index.
ISBN 1-887896-39-2
1. Alternative medicine. 2. Indians of North America—Medicine. 3. Shamanism. I. Title.
R733 .P396 2002
615.5—dc21 2002015427

Design: Charles Alexander   Illustrations: Cynthia Miller

Printed in Canada
10 9 8 7 6 5 4 3 2 1

Disclaimer: This book is designed to offer items of general interest to the reader. It is not intended to address individual problems or to offer medical or legal advice. If you believe you are ill, have any conditions described in this book, or experience symptoms, consult your local health care practitioner. The author specifically disclaims any liability, loss, or risk, personal or indirectly, from the use and application of any of the contents of this book.

Note: Throughout this book, the names of actual patients and healers and their identifying characteristics have been changed in order to maintain confidentiality.

Various terms including "American Indian," "Native American," "Tribal," "Native Nations," "First Nations," and "Native Peoples" are currently part of English language usage. All are used by indigenous inhabitants of the Americas, and so all are used interchangeably in this book. To avoid occasional ambiguity the word "Native" is capitalized in expressions referring to Native healers and healing, as is the word "White" when it refers to ethnicity.

Acknowledgements: Thanks to Cindy Levack, Hannah Rowland, Jennie Norris, and Jolene Fishel for invaluable word processing assistance; to Ross Humphreys, Susan Lowell, and Ron Foreman for editorial guidance on our journey from an idea to a book; to David Lynn and William Inboden for permission to cite their Recovery Together program; and to Marissa Peate for her poem in Chapter 10. Certain materials in this book are adapted from the author's prior publications: *On the Serendipity Road* (with James Hine), *Genome II,* and *Cold Peace.* Thanks also to Luci Tapahonso for permission to reprint her poem, "There is Nothing Quite Like This" (© 1987 by Luci Tapahonso) and to Christopher Logue for his untitled poem, reprinted on p. 175 (© 1969 by Christopher Logue).

To all who seek healing—

the healers and the healed—

of mind, body, and spirit.

May this story give you strength.

Contents

Prelude

There is Nothing Quite Like This

a cream-colored horse
galloping in the sunrise

circling to the east
four times
in the pink morning sky
look, the streaks of purple
in gray clouds

the horse runs hard, raising dust
the dawn is still
we watch
there is nothing quite like this to see

the rider: straw hat and rawhide whip
he yells out on the west side
of the hooghan
he yells out four times on the west
hey! hey! hey! hey!

they have heard
the spirits are coming
they are coming now

the western sky
a matrix of quick lightning streaks
in dark, dark clouds

the lukachukai mountains are damp
dripping with rain
even from here in the desert, we know.

we watch
the cream-colored horse and
the rider with the strong morning yell

take heed,
they circle four times
around the hooghan
they have come
the spirits singing and healing

we are better now for seeing this
a cream-colored horse galloping in circles

the pink sunrise in the warm desert morning

already at 6 am, it's hot and we return
to the fires to cook and
catch up on the latest stories around this area.

—Luci Tapahonso

Lukachukai: A locality on the Navajo Reservation in northern Arizona.

hooghan: Traditional Navajo dwelling, often spelled "hogan."

Navajo writer Luci Tapahonso is the author of five collections of prose and poetry. She is a professor of creative writing and American Indian Studies at the University of Arizona.

Introduction

Native Healing: four sacred paths to health

Knowledge is the mother of science. Opinion is the mother of ignorance.
—Hippocrates (460-377 B.C.)

For centuries Native healers have improved health and changed lives. And today more than ever, Native healers, in combination with Western medicine, offer one of the most effective methods to balance physical with emotional and spiritual healing.

This is a book for everyone, whatever your race, religion, or ethnicity. Maybe you are seeking health and well-being. Possibly you are exploring the power of spirituality and healing. Perhaps you have asked if your physical symptoms and hoped-for recovery are affected by your state of mind. Whatever the reason, you will be rewarded with answers that will enrich your life.

More than ever before, understanding other cultures is essential to our well-being. As you read this book, you'll experience a unique vision of how to heal, live, and recover that will forever change the way you think about the world.

Here you'll meet many Native healers including Annie, a Diné (Navajo) medicine woman, and Joe, a Yakima practitioner who knows how to "go into the light" with his patients. You'll read the remarkable story of Rachel, who finds herself sitting in a circle in a sweat lodge, hoping that this last resort will relieve her pain. You'll read the history of Manco Capa, the great Peruvian healer who treats toothache and lassos the sun, and you will meet Skip, a Cherokee doctor and fisherman—and a Dartmouth M.D. You'll watch as a

Tohono O'odham midwife delivers a baby, and you'll listen to the poignant words of dying patients. You will live through a day in the life of a modern medical practitioner who relies on some ancient methods (me). Interspersed throughout the book, these case histories illuminate many aspects of healing in the twenty-first century, including its dark side.

Why bother when we have modern technology?

Native Healing: Four Sacred Paths to Health is not about abandoning effective Western medicine. I certainly haven't. Trained in the field of medicine at Dartmouth Medical School and in public health at Harvard University, I currently hold academic appointments in both of those areas at the University of Arizona College of Medicine and College of Public Health in Tucson, where I am also a practicing physician specializing in community medicine. I have served as a medical and public health worker in Africa and Latin America as well as the United States. My interest in Native healing has been growing ever since I first worked as a medical student on the Navajo Reservation in 1980. But it probably began much earlier, for I've always taken great pride in my descent through my mother from the Mohawk and Onondaga people of upstate New York—two of the Six Nations of the Iroquois.

Rather than abandoning Western medical practices, this book is about using other methods either to enrich modern medicine or to find answers when standard treatments don't work. Native healing is not only about medicine of the past, but it offers a new paradigm for the future, too. It recognizes the intense interaction between mind and body, and it promotes the power of community, spirituality, and healing. Though there is an increasing concern with emotional well-being, modern physicians are primarily interested in the physical components of their patients. But having diabetes or other conditions is far more than measuring or adjusting blood sugar. Numerous health benefits occur if an individual's culture, family, and beliefs are woven into prevention and treatment.

Like herbal remedies, isn't this just a fad?

Open a newspaper or turn on a television, and you'll predictably be informed about the latest health innovation. Alternative medicine, holistic health, herbal remedies, and spiritual healing are promoted as recent improvements over modern medicine. All have been practiced by Native Peoples for thousands of years.

Consider herbal or botanical medications. One in four modern prescription drugs contains an ingredient from a flowering plant. One in five plants has a documented medical use. For example, digitalis is a commonly used heart medicine originally derived from the foxglove plant, *Digitalis purpurea.* Interestingly, the botanical substance was safer than the pure chemical digitalis because other components in the plant provided early warning signs of an overdose.

Similarly, all the chemically pure, anti-aging antioxidants that vendors urge us to buy, such as catalase, glutathione, and SOD, are compounds created internally by the body. But when an external source is ingested, it is made useless by normal digestion. Rather than eating pure "antioxidants," a better method, in most cases, is to eat an adequate amount of vegetables and fruits that provide dozens of health-promoting ingredients, not just a select few.

Antioxidant-rich foods

Vegetables: beets, broccoli, Brussels sprouts, corn, eggplant, kale, onions, red bell peppers, and spinach*

Fruits: blueberries, cherries, kiwis, oranges, plums, prunes, raisins, raspberries, red grapes, red grapefruit, and strawberries

*Alfalfa sprouts are rich in antioxidants, but recent Centers for Disease Control and Prevention (CDC) reports describe food contamination from certain suppliers.

Why four sacred paths?

Four has a special significance in tribal cultures. Quartets of symbols resonate in Native healing: Four sacred directions are used to help the ill recover; healers compose herbal formulas from four strong medicines and balance them according to individual need; and four sacred materials are essential to many healing practices and are also evident in weavings, sculpture, painting, and jewelry. The Iroquois built their longhouses oriented to the sacred four directions. Even tribes are sometimes divided into fourths: the traditional Tsimshian of the Pacific Northwest were organized into four clans.

North:
The spirit runs
through the body —
spirituality and healing

West:
Restoring
healing balance —
Native healers

East:
The power
of relationships —
healing as a group activity

South:
The healing life cycle —
beginnings, endings,
and the next world

What does each of the four sections/directions include?

Each starts with a case—a patient's story that illustrates that section's theme.

Each uses quotes—Native healers' comments as pullouts in the text that interpret certain healing practices, how they are used to restore balance and well-being, and why they work.

Each offers practical suggestions and personal healing habits you can use to maximize Native healing values in your own life.

Each presents visual images for each of the four themes in the text.

- The Sun that brings warmth
- The Wind that brings the rain clouds
- The Rain that gives life-giving moisture
- The Earth that gives nourishment

Each provides books, articles, and websites for additional information.

North: the spirit runs through the body—spirituality and healing

The sacred way of life or *wak'a* guides Native healers. Taken from the Quechua language, which is still spoken in the Andes by descendants of the Incas, the term "wak'a" has no exact equivalent in our English vocabulary. "Sacredness," "stewardship of our bodies and Nature's bounty," and "self esteem" are all inadequate. Native healers do not separate the body from the mind or soul. This discussion covers:

Finding and remedying the true cause of illness
Creating a vision of well-being
Healing a broken spirit

East: the power of relationships—healing as a group activity

In contrast to many modern practitioners of integrative and alternative medicine, who often limit their health advice to individuals, Native healers explore and promote the powerful effects of family and community on personal health. This section explores:

The importance of ceremony and family tradition as healing agents
Practical ways of healing and connecting with the community and family

West: restoring healing balance—Native healers

Native healers see patients as health "partners" who actively participate with their community in their recovery. Topics reviewed include:

Choosing widely and wisely from Native and Western medicine
Healthful living, balance, and purification in a connected world
Blessings, songs, chants, and cures

South: the healing life cycle—beginnings, endings, and the next world

For Native healers wellness is restored when mind, body, spirit, and community are in harmony within a natural cycle. Among the themes discussed are:

Childbirth and beginnings
Grief and endings
Space and place in health (as expressed by the Navajo word *hozho*)

North: hospital bed underwater?

Native healers have traditionally incorporated the total person—physical, spiritual, mental—in their understanding of healing. Modern health care facilities have supported chaplain services, including Native healers in some places. Some are going a step further and adding baptisms for the seriously ill, as in a recent case in Pikeville, Kentucky.

> *" 'It's a comfort to the family members and to the patient to know they can have this baptism done before any surgeries or before any complications that they fear might arise,' said the Rev. Mark Walz, chaplain of Pikeville Methodist Hospital, which recently installed two baptisteries.*
>
> *"Doris Gillmen, 76, who suffers from lung cancer, was baptized in the Pikeville hospital by being lowered on bed sheets into water. 'Her face just lit up after she was baptized. She raised her arm like she was praising the Lord,' her daughter Esther Gibson said.*
>
> *"Joel Green, dean of the school of theology at Asbury Theological Seminary in Wilmore, Kentucky, said he considers the trend good for medical care. 'It suggests something about dealing with people as whole persons, not just bodies over here and soul over there … It places an emphasis on the health of the whole person.'*
>
> *"Furman Hewitt, director of the Baptist House at Duke Divinity School in Durham, N.C., said, 'Hospital baptisteries are an interesting twist to the push in the medical field to deal with the total person—physical, mental, and spiritual.' "*
>
> *(Associated Press, July 20, 2001)*

Truth in advertising?

One of the myths of modern living is that there must be an immediate solution to every ill. Take a drug or other treatment, and your problem will be instantly solved. Most of us have attempted a self-improvement program or tried a new fad, only to be disappointed when the results never materialized or we reverted to old destructive habits.

We fantasize that if only we could find the right healer (or pill or marriage partner or neighborhood), or beat the competition or foreign enemy, then everything would be all right. If only we knew the secret, we could succeed. If there are "secrets" to Native healing, they are:

North: Native healing is a partnership with yourself. When things don't get better, the solution may be inside your own head, within your soul. Native healers believe you have everything you need inside you.

The healing spirit runs through the body

East: Native healing is a partnership with others—family members, community. A Native healer once paraphrased Abe Lincoln to me: "You can heal some things all of the time," the healer said, "and you can heal all things some of the time, but you can't heal everything all the time alone." Everyone needs a coach, a family, a community.

The healing power of relationships

West: Native healing is a partnership between the healer and you. It is just as important to become the right patient as it is to find the right healer or healing. Native healing requires active participation by the one to be healed.

Restoring healing balance

South: Native healing is a partnership for life. It has its beginnings and endings, and although the middle sometimes isn't easy, especially after your initial enthusiasm has faded, there is fulfillment and healing harmony at the end.

The healing life cycle

Are you wondering if all this isn't some hoax or superstitious babble? Surely a licensed medical practitioner and professor of medicine and public health wouldn't give credence to ancient practices conducted by chanting Indians using herbs? Is it the actual practice or the belief in the practice that heals? In the next section we'll discover how a Harvard-trained physician came to some surprising findings about the benefits of Native healing.

East: healthy heart or mind or 'hood?

Native healers have long recognized the influence of community on health. Here's a surprising and confirmatory discovery from modern medicine. What has the greatest effect on the differences in heart disease between rich and poor neighborhoods: income, education, occupation, smoking, physical activity, diabetes, high blood pressure, type of cholesterol, weight or body mass index?

The answer, based on research in Britain and across the United States, may surprise you. High-income Blacks in poor neighborhoods had better hearts than lower-income Whites in richer neighborhoods even though both had the same income, education, lifestyle, risk factors, and access to health care.

Something beyond genetics, lifestyle, behavior, income, or health care disparities affects health. Is it envy, looking over our shoulders at others, or lack of control that leads to bad health disparities? Researchers suggest two areas for intervention, both of which have long been known by Native healers: "enhancing the social and psychological resources of individual people, and improving the quality of neighborhoods and communal life."

Added M.G. Marmot, one of the authors of an important study: "My own view is that the mind is a crucial gateway through which social influences affect physiology to cause disease. The mind may work through effects on health-related behavior, such as smoking, eating, drinking, physical activity, or risk taking, or it may act through effects on neuroendocrine or immune mechanisms."

West: health in head and heart

Heart disease is the number-one killer in industrialized countries. Could the reason be inside our heads? Native healing, like folk wisdom, promotes a balanced, positive outlook as a powerful tool to prevent heart and other disease. Recent research provides confirmatory evidence that this is correct. The Veterans Affairs Normative Aging Study, which has examined 2,280 men since 1963, found that those who were pessimistic, based on the Minnesota Multiphasic Personality Inventory (MMPI), had twice as much heart disease as the optimists.

Resources

Acheson D. Independent inquiry into inequalities in health report. London: The Stationery Office, 1998.

Beckman KB, Ames BN. The free radical theory of aging matures. Physiological reviews, 1998; 78:547-581.

Brown K. The quest to beat aging: a radical proposal. Scientific American, 2000;11:39-43.

Diez-Roux AV, Stein O Merkin S, Arnett D, et al. Neighborhood of residence and incidence of coronary heart disease. N Engl J Med 2001;345:99-106.

Geronimus AT, Bound J, Waidmann TA, Hillemeier MM, Burns PB. Excess mortality among blacks and whites in the United States. N Engl J Med 1996;335:1552-8.

Griffin JM, Fuhrer R, Stansfeld SA, Marmot MG. The importance of low control at work and home on depression and anxiety: do these vary by gender and class? Soc Sci Med (in press).

Joseph A et al. Reversals of age-related declines in neuronal signal transduction, cognitive, and motor behavioral deficits with blueberry, spinach or strawberry dietary supplementation. Neurosci, 1999;19:8114-8121.

Kubzansky LD, Sparrow D, Vokonas P, Kawachi L. Is the glass half emply or half full? A prospective study of optimism and coronary heart disease in the normative aging study. Psychosom Med. 2001;63:910-6.

Hoyce CR, Welldon RM. The objective efficacy of prayer: a double blind clinical trial. J Chron Dis. 1965; 18:367-377.

King DE, Buchwick B. Beliefs and attitudes of hospital inpatients about faith healing and prayers. J Fam Pract. 1994;39:349-352.

Lynch JW, Davey Smith G, Kaplan GA, House JS. Income inequality and mortality: importance to health of individual income, psychosocial environment, or material conditions. BMJ 2000;320:1200-4.

MacIntyre S, MacIver S, Sooman A. Area, class and health: should we be focusing on places or people? J Soc Policy 1993;22:213-34.

Marmot MG, Bosma J, Hemingway H, Brunner E, Stanfeld S. Contribution of job control and other risk factors to social variations in coronary heart disease incidence. Lancet 1997;350:235-9.

Marmot MG, Shipley MJ, Rose G. Inequalities in death—specific explanations of a general pattern? Lancet 1984;1:1003-6.

Marmot M, Wilkinson RG. Psychosocial and material pathways in the relation between income and health: a response to Lynch et al. BMJ 2001;322:1233-6.

McCord C, Freeman HP. Excess mortality in Harlem. New Engl J Med 1990;322:173-7.

McEwen BS. Protective and damaging effects of stress mediators. N Engl J Med 1998;338:171-9.

Murray CJL, Michaud MC, McKenna M, Marks J U.S. patterns of mortality by county and race: 1965-1994. Cambridge, MA.: Harvard Center for Population and Development Studies, 1998;1-97.

Pappas G, Queen S, Hadden W, Fisher G. The increasing disparity in mortality between socioeconomic groups in the United States 1960 and 1986. N Engl J Med 1993;329:1139.

Parks TL, et al. Extension of drosophila lifespan by overexpression of human SOD1 in motor neurons. Nature Genetics, 1998;19:171-174.

Sen AK. Development as freedom. New York: Knopf, 1999.

Stansfeld SA, Head J, Marmot MG. Explaining social class differences in depression and well-being. Soc Psychiatry Psychiatr Epidemiol 1998;33:1-9.

The World Bank. World Development Report 1999/2000. New York: Oxford University Press, 2000.

1

Listening with Your Heart

Wind blows, but never moves a mountain, until it brings life-giving rain that melts the earth away.
— Navajo Healer

You can't teach anybody anything, not anything of lasting importance anyway, unless you love 'em.
— Martin Luther King, Jr.

Ever have an experience that was so striking that years later you can still hear the sounds and picture the scene, place, and people? Here's one that occurred while I was serving as a senior medical student in the intensive care unit (ICU) at the Tuba City Hospital on the Navajo Reservation in Arizona.

"Get his blood pressure down now, before he has a stroke!" barked the attending physician, my supervisor. His handsome thirtyish face remained calm amidst the crisis.

Old Man Hosteen, an elderly Navajo man—a tough old rooster whose time had come—lay comatose in the ICU bed like a chocolate mummy swaddled in bandages. A silver and turquoise bracelet, a blood pressure cuff, and a medusa of nonfunctioning intravenous lines competed for space on his arm. His blood pressure was in the stratosphere, and we weren't able to do anything about it. I've found there is something surreal, otherworldly, when you're this close to death. The angels wait for a misstep, an error, or sometimes just an inevitability.

Old Man Hosteen's life depended on my getting his intravenous line into his vein and his medicine restarted, I thought, as the nurse hung his medication on the intravenous pole and waited for me. I prayed for an easy-to-find vein, or one that wouldn't roll away from the point of my catheter. He had neither. His veins were playing hide-and-seek under his dark skin, made leathery from years of harsh desert sun and chapping wind. The metallic warning beep of the blood pressure monitor alarm as well as the nurse's complaint ("Aren't you ready yet?") collided against my concentration. I'd give it one last try before admitting defeat. Suddenly, the catheter found its way into a vein. A backsplash of Navajo blood, dusky ochre from low oxygen, confirmed I was in. I turned to open up the stopcock to release his medicine when a man who smelled like a musty campfire blocked my view—a Native healer, I learned later.

"Can you please move?" I warned him more than asked him.

"Need room," he countered, as he spread out a woolen gray and red rug on the linoleum floor of the ICU room.

"What are you doing?" I said. "You're going to have to leave."

"The wind may blow, but it will never move the mountain," he answered, with a serene, not-of-this-world look on his face.

"Please ask him to stop annoying my patient!" I pleaded with the nurse.

The nurses hushed me as the man sprinkled cornmeal on the four corners of Hosteen's bed and began a high-pitched chant. Certain that these high jinks would worsen Hosteen's blood pressure, I checked it again. It had fallen to normal! Thank God for modern medicine, I thought, until I realized the catheterized vein had exploded—no blood pressure-lowering drug had gone in, after all. Old Man Hosteen later said he was going towards a light when he heard the Native healer's chant, and that it was those soothing words that brought him back to life.

He was right.

A long bumpy journey

This was my first experience with Native healing. Was it an unproven, superstitious, non-FDA-approved distraction, or something else? For me, understanding the benefits of Native healing was a long bumpy journey. As a medical student I was being trained to take an efficient history of each patient under my care so I could order the correct tests and start the right medicines. I found I could hear hearts with my stethoscope, but that I was missing a great deal by not listening with *my* heart. How so?

Hate a patient?

It may be hard to believe, but doctors hate patients. Oh, not all the time, some hardly ever, but the honest ones will admit that at least once in their careers they have had a dreadful experience with, and a longstanding grudge against, a person seeking their help. Such patients are much like your toughest teachers. You complain about them, but you also learn the most from them. So it was with me not long after the Native healer incident in the ICU.

Mr. and Mrs. Backstabber

Mrs. J had been admitted to the Tuba City hospital for chest pain, a condition that kills half a million Americans each year. All her tests were negative, but she continued to have a sensation of "stabbing knives" in her sternum, or breastbone. Her husband would faithfully sit by her bed while we carefully explained the normal results of all her diagnostic studies. The J's were middle-aged, well-dressed members of the Navajo bourgeoisie, the type of patients all doctors think they would like in their practice. Except . . . Mrs. J had an annoying habit of removing her many bracelets, applying dollops of overly-scented hand cream, and asking, "Now what did you say?" instead of listening. Mr. J, a refrigerator-sized man with a knuckle-cracking handshake, seemed like a kettle ready to boil over. He would blurt out words, abruptly stop in mid-sentence, and irritably mutter, "Never mind," when urged to finish his thoughts.

One morning on our daily rounds, we asked if either had any questions, answered them, and left to attend to others far sicker. As soon as we did, Mr. J shambled out of the room, cornered us in the hallway, and demanded, "Now tell me what's really going on with my wife!" We repeated the same information and added that we had nothing to withhold from either him or his wife.

At that moment the floor nurse cut us short. Mrs. J was having chest pain again—"the worst ever." We scurried back to her room, reevaluated her and repeated her electrocardiogram. Everything was normal. This scenario occurred three days in a row. And each day all assurances to Mr. J that we weren't holding back information were always accepted without disagreement or rebuttal.

On the fourth day I was paged by the hospital administrator. "What in the hell are you doing to Mrs. J?" he wanted to know. "She and her husband have filed a formal complaint that you're keeping secrets from her ... and *that* makes her chest feel worse. Are you helping or hurting her?" His words stung because in my mind we had done all we could.

I was so angry that I ran to Mrs. J's room to set her straight. I confronted Mrs. J about her complaint and repeated my prior statement that we were sharing all information.

"Then why does my husband follow you out into the hallway to talk with you? I'm dying, aren't I, and you're afraid to tell me?"

Just then Mr. J appeared. He said, "Doctor, we just want the truth."

Obviously something was going on that wasn't in my medical textbook. We had followed the best medical practice, had spoken with both members of the family truthfully. Yet I was in trouble, and my evaluation for the rotation was in jeopardy, all because of Mr. and Mrs. J.

"Look, you two, you're the problem here!" I said, raising my voice for emphasis. "From now on, Mr. J, no hallway conversations. We only speak to both of you together—no more separate conversations."

"How am I going to know what's going on with my wife?" he shot back.

The nurses later told me I yelled my answer: "By listening to what we tell you when you're together!"

I pretended I was being paged and excused myself from the room ... and guess who followed me out for a private conversation, and whose wife had another severe bout of chest pain? At this point I was ready to give Mr. J sudden face pain with my fist when the Navajo healer shuffled by. He looked me up and down through glasses mended at the nose bridge with masking tape and repeated his prior admonition.

"Proving you are right is like the wind trying to push over a mountain," he said. He smiled crookedly through a file of missing teeth and walked away.

"Great," I thought. "Everybody is against me: the hospital administrator, the patients, the nurses, and even a medicine man who has nothing to teach *me*—the product of higher education!" Or could he?

More than I would ever guess. Little did I know that the hallway meeting would be a defining, life-changing event in my medical career and my approach to healing.

Warm science

Later I reviewed the day's events with my attending physician. He had also been present with Old Man Hosteen, our ICU patient with the dangerous high blood pressure that returned to normal when the Native healer began to chant. My attending was an impeccably-trained internist from back East, now practicing in the harsh extremity of the West called Dinetah, or Navajoland. Why was he there? The reason for his service among us was the subject of intense speculation when the hospital staff found time to gossip.

"What can a witch doctor offer that we can't?" I asked. I felt this was a cheap shot against people with whom I shared bloodlines (my mother is part Mohawk and Onondaga, two of the six Iroquois tribes), but I still couldn't understand why some Indians would insist on old methods when modern medicine was clearly better.

"They provide what we used to offer," he said reflectively. "It may seem strange, but before we had modern technology and medicines, doctors were better liked than they are now, even though they could cure a lot less."

"How could that be?" I asked, with a growing fear that even my attending was betraying me.

"Back then, doctors knew their patients, lived in their neighborhoods, knew who was strong and who wasn't, listened instead of tested, reassured instead of frightened. Native healers still do."

"But they had so few cures!"

"They had the 'cure' of reassurance that even if an illness caused body functions—even life itself—to change, eternal things would never desert them, like their family, traditions, and spiritual beliefs."

The next day I searched for the right words for Mr. and Mrs. J. After all, I was a newly minted medical professional and they were an inconvenience, a distraction. But were they really, or were the J's the reason the whole medical establishment existed in the first place? I decided to try it the Navajo way, no blowing wind to move the immovable mountain. Instead of a confrontation and an attempt to prove I was right, smarter, and more rational, I sat down with the J's, asked for a fresh start, and started with general open-ended questions.

"What's going on in your life? How is this affecting you? What troubles you the most? If we could change one thing, what would it be?" I asked.

The answers were surprising then, but not so in retrospect. I learned that Mr. J had a habit of concealing painful or awkward information from Mrs. J, hoping to spare her from grief, but she always learned the truth anyhow. Now that she was in the hospital, she feared his secret conversations with us concealed a terrible secret.

It seemed that when Mr. J was eighteen he had lost his mother to cancer in the days when information was withheld from younger family members to "protect" them. He regretted that the doctors hadn't told him his mother was terminally ill. If they had, he would have spent more time with her and delayed joining U.S. Army Basic Training across the continent from the Navajo Reservation. He feared that we, the medical team, were hiding equally serious information about his wife. I promised him that times change and we would keep him and his wife informed about all medical results, no matter how serious. Since I was going to keep my promise, he had to keep one also—no wife-scaring private conversations with us anymore. He agreed.

Native healing under my skin

"How'd it go with Mr. and Mrs. J?" my attending asked warily. I could tell by the way his jaw had set hard that he expected the worst. I reviewed my approach and apparent success. He applauded my decision but seemed uneasy that I had attributed my success to the example of the Native healer. Perhaps he was afraid I had gone too far with his advice.

"Remember not to generalize," he said. "He is just one healer, from one tribe. There are 560 Indian nations, each with its own healing methods. Of course you have lots of options to choose from."

There are now 561 Indian nations, since the Yaqui, the tribe who live closest to my present-day home, weren't recognized at that time.

"But isn't it our job to guide them to modern medicine?" This was my last attempt to preserve the medical world where I had been educated. "What about anesthesia and antibiotics—what if we only had Indian medicine? Wouldn't a lot of people have died?"

"Don't forget that Indians found natural pain relievers and antibiotics many years before we did. A plant called *Spirea ulmaria*, or queen-of-the-meadow, contained the chemical predecessor to aspirin, and cinchona tree bark gave us the antimicrobial quinine." He lowered his voice: "Sometimes we don't have all the answers." Then he put his head in his hands, sighed, and volunteered, "I've even seen a healer."

I must have given him the look of someone who has just realized he is having dinner with a psychotic.

He explained: "I just couldn't figure out what I wanted to do with my life ... I was losing sleep, overeating ... that's why I came out West." And then he described a Navajo sing—a healing ceremony—that he had participated in.

"Ever been inside during a storm when the wind bangs branches against the building, rafters creak, and rain pelts the windows, but inside all is warm and safe—that's a sing." He went on, as his eyes stared through me to a distant cherished place.

"The chanting seeps under your skin, gets inside you to your core. Suddenly your pulse is in rhythm with the singers' beat, and then you seem to float free of worry or fear." He opened his hands palms up as if he was holding on to a great truth too large to contain. "The simplicity of the moment is overwhelming. You realize you are among people free of ambition for power or wealth, who are keepers of an ancient wisdom. They know how to live a life filled with meaning, not superficiality or self-absorption."

"Is that what the Navajos mean when they say 'walk in beauty'?" I asked.

"Precisely. Those words are a blessing, a hope that you will always remember and hold on to what is truly meaningful. It's goofy, but I felt that the healer reached inside of me to a part I hadn't listened to for a long time. It helped me to get back on track. Don't mention it to the other staff," he said, winking conspiratorially.

I thought if someone as "together" as my attending had seen a Native healer, maybe there was something to it. But he was right. I had had only a momentary experience with just one healer, from a single tribe. Where to go from here?

"Since there are half a thousand Indian nations, each with different languages and traditions, how does one ever make sense of Native healing?" I asked.

He answered: "In a symphony there are many instruments that make different sounds, but there are unifying themes ... and beautiful music."

And so it was with Native healing. It was up to me to discover the unity in the diversity.

Four commonalities—sacred paths to healing

Over many years as a practicing physician I've learned that in spite of individual and tribal variations, there are four common elements that can be summarized in both a written and a graphical format. (Native healers respect different learning styles—some patients are more visual, others auditory.) The four sacred paths work together to create a harmony of health, and like good musical conductors, Native healers may use all or part of their repertoire. Each of these four themes or sacred paths to healing is reviewed in later chapters, along with practical tips to help you apply them to your own life. Every healing is a journey. Each journey needs a map, a set of guidelines to help the traveler stay on the path and avoid a crash. So as you read, watch for the essential road signals to follow.

2

Manco Capa's Healing Class: a history

Life is not a matter of holding good cards, but rather of having bad cards and playing them well.

—Robert Louis Stevenson (1850-1894)

"What makes you sick?" I asked in the best Quechua I could manage.

Years had passed since I first met the Navajo healer at Hosteen's bedside. Now I stood high on a mountain in another continent, trying to teach a health class to a group of young Peruvians. Quechua was once the language of the ancient Inca empire. Nowadays it is spoken in the six Andean countries of South America by thirteen million people, sometimes including me.

The class looked at me silently. A fly buzzed into the room, and its hum made the silence more evident. Outside the open front door of the newly built secondary-school classroom (constructed with clay, water, straw, heat, and the ready hands of the Lower Vilcabamba villagers), the white alpaca that always hung around the village children chewed loudly on *quichnah* grass.

Inside my head I could hear the glib words I had spoken so many times in other health classes in other places: Ninety-five percent of health can be taught by someone with a high school degree. Wash your hands before you eat and after you defecate. Keep hot foods hot and cold foods cold, cover your mouth before you cough or sneeze, eat lots of fruits and vegetables, brush your teeth after every meal, drink clean water. I could just lecture and give a test. That's what they did at my secondary school, didn't they?

But all I said was: "Well, any ideas?" More silence. This was it. I turned to collect my pack—.

"Spirits," said a small voice from near the back. The boy looked about twelve years old, but he was probably older. Starvation kept you small.

"What does a spirit mean to you?" I asked.

"They are inside you. They make you sick."

"What do they look like?"

"You can't see them."

"Germs." I said the word in English; I didn't know the Quechua equivalent. "That is what makes you sick."

"What do they look like?"

"They're so small you can't see them." I wished I had a microscope.

"If you can't see them, then they must be spirits," challenged the boy. Others giggled. These people weren't backward; they were intensely curious and logical.

"Let's try it another way. What else makes you sick?"

"Diarrhea."

"What causes diarrhea?"

"Bad food ... Bad water ... " The answers came in a torrent.

"That is why you shouldn't poop in the river," I said. "If you do you can get sick and die young."

The twelve-year-old spoke again. "My great-grandfather is seventy-seven winters old and he always drinks from the river."

This wasn't a health class; it was a debating squad, I thought.

"Listen up," I said in exasperation. "You need to know this stuff for the test. Now the internal structure of the abscessed tooth ... "

The classroom of young students suddenly stirred. Their countryman, the famous healer Manco Capa, had dropped in for another unexpected visit to Lower Vilcabamba Village. Manco's features were classic Inca: hair still thick as raven feathers, a proud aquiline nose, and eyes distinguished not by their color but by their intensity, even behind the lenses of his spectacles. At five and a half feet tall he was a big man for his race, with the broad chest of someone born and raised at high elevations.

"Oh, hi, Manco," I said. "Class, say, '*Alianchu*'"

This is a Quecha greeting somewhat like "Hello."

"*Aliyami*," said the chorus of voices. (This is the proper response to "*Alianchu*.")

"No, don't answer me with '*aliyami*' when I say '*alianchu*,' say it to Dr. Capa."

"*Aliyami*," they repeated again.

I shrugged. Communication problems once again! "I'm trying to lecture them on healthy teeth," I explained.

"Well, Peate," Manco said, "how well would you do if you were lectured to all day and never got to practice?"

"Crummy."

"Try this." Manco turned to the class. "Anyone ever have a sore tooth?"

"I did. The *bruja* (witch) cursed me," announced one girl.

"My mother had one and the *curandero* (local healer) pulled it out," said another child, who showed off the toothless gap in her own mouth. "He told her, 'One day all teeth go bad,' so he pulled all of them at the same time."

"I have a bad tooth right now," said the first girl, in obvious discomfort.

"Class, let's look at her teeth and see if we can figure out what's wrong," said Manco.

They dropped their notebooks and huddled around their classmate María. She opened her mouth slowly. Her jaw was swollen and a faint redness radiated around the left cheek.

Manco said, "What do you see?"

"She is red ... swollen ... she burns like fire ... "They all spoke in chorus.

"What else?"

"Her breath stinks like the latrine!" added one boy. All of them laughed. María jabbed her elbow in her critical classmate's side and tried to laugh too, then stopped. It hurt too much.

"Redness, swelling, fever, and bad breath ... my apologies, María. What is wrong?"

"Germs," said one.

"Anything else?" asked Manco.

"She has an abscess, an infection," said another.

"What caused it?" I asked, warming to Manco's Socratic approach.

"She has a *nuña* bean caught in her gum," declared one observant boy. The high-protein *nuña* or pop bean has a kernel like popcorn that can become lodged between gum and tooth.

"Let's look and see." María opened again wider. Manco examined her gums gingerly. The girl was in pain.

"Got it." He removed a piece of *nuña* bean kernel with a forceps and showed it to the group.

"María, gargle with salt water three times a day. Two pinches in a glass, like this. And take echinacea three times a day. I'll give it to your mother. Tomorrow you will show the class and they will practice, too."

María nodded. "How do I prevent it?"

"Smart question. Use a toothbrush," I offered.

"These people can't afford toothbrushes," Manco reminded me. "Use a stick, like this," he volunteered, and he demonstrated with a green twig he had hidden in his pocket.

"Class outside," ordered Manco. We followed a parade of gangly feet and legs too long for bodies. Manco climbed up the mountainside among the students. His legs pumped like machines at the 9,000-foot altitude, moving with conditioned ease like someone with half his fifty-seven years.

"Pick a twig, pull off the leaves . . . not a whole tree, María, just a twig," said Manco as he swirled the stick against the teeth in his mouth. "Now scrub your teeth like this," he said, which actually sounded like: "Nah schub yah heeth lak thith."

The students followed along while I watched, a little short of breath from thin air and my usual amazement at Manco Capa.

The man who brushed his teeth with the twig was the leader of all the Quechua-speaking healers. An expert in herbal medicine, Manco Capa had taught in some of the great universities of the world. He was also the Sapa Inca, representative of the Sun God on Earth.

Each year in June at Machu Picchu he conducted an ancient ritual on the winter solstice in the Southern Hemisphere, the day the Sun was farthest from the Earth. He climbed in the icy dawn to the sundial of the Temple of the Sun, a gray thumb of somber stone. There, like his grandfathers before him, Manco removed a medallion of Inca gold he had hidden under a fold in his tunic and reverently positioned it on the stone sundial, which after half a millennium remained in perfect condition, a testament to Inca craftsmanship. Each winter solstice the Sapa Inca must prevent the sun from escaping by symbolically roping the gold disk to the sundial.

At the same time Manco wondered why he bothered. He had shared some of his concerns with me. During the past decades man's pollution had trapped Inti the Sun God's heat in the atmosphere, creating what the Winter People (the tribes of Europe and their mixed-blood clan the Americans) called the "greenhouse effect." And Raingiver had held back the rains from the scorched Earth. Paradoxically, as the Earth heated, more water evaporated from the oceans and caused unusual precipitation, such as hail at higher, colder altitudes. The forests filled with medicinal plants were fast disappearing.

Still, Manco knew the world hungered for more than food. The West with all its wealth (even its ghetto dwellers were kings by Andean standards) was afflicted by a famine of the soul, a lack of wak'a. Substance abuse, ennui, waste, and moral decline chewed at the spiritually-dead, fat flanks of the West like greedy maggots. Wak'a had no translation in the Winter People's language, according to Manco. The West sought truth, revered individualism and worshipped freedom, yet there was never anything the Andean people needed to be free from, no truth to chase, no community to separate from. Each possessed a personal reservoir of wak'a: an illuminating essence as bright as Inti's celestial flame. No matter how poor his people were in material goods, the strength of wak'a, the spirit-community that his people valued more than life itself, held against all storms. Even when they were sick and starving, their wak'a still burned. But many had sacrificed their wak'a in the Western marketplace, inheriting greed and excess without the balance of reason and temperance. In the end they were left with the ills of the West without the protection of wak'a.

Tossing his twig away, Manco looked upward and fixed the burning star of Inti briefly in his gaze. Great gobbets of hydrogen atoms fused with other hydrogen atoms to create helium and energy, hummed the scientist part of his mind. Two parts make one. Unity. Energy. Wak'a.

Manco turned to me. "The Winter People misnamed physics," he said. "They should have called it life."

Meanwhile the village children laughed and cleaned their teeth, and the white alpaca grazed nearby.

A note on the history of Manco Capa

Manco Capa's story captures the situation of many Native healers, respected and effective in their communities, capable of bridging the divide between ancient curing practices and modern medicine, yet pitted against enormous adverse forces—physical, political, and cultural—that range from the ill effects of malnutrition to those of urbanization and global warming. For example, their sources for healing plants are disappearing due to local and global circumstances. I once had a patient ask, "What's the big deal about saving the rain forest and a bunch of plants nobody has heard of? Don't we have plenty of pharmaceutical companies that can cook up any drug we want?"

Regrettably, many drug companies are in the business of creating look-alike drugs rather than breakthrough ones. For example, one company will design a successful cholesterol lowering drug. The others will try to duplicate that success by simply altering a single atom on that drug, creating a patentable product that they can sell, but one that lacks any new contribution to healing. The truly groundbreaking, but riskier, drug possibilities are frequently ignored in the pursuit of copycat drugs.

So where shall we find revolutionary healing agents? In Manco Capa's back yard. Native healers across the globe have been experimenting with herbal remedies for centuries. Unfortunately, plant species are vanishing at an alarming rate. To counteract that trend the University of Arizona College of Pharmacy has a major research center led by Dr. Barbara Timmermann that is devoted to capturing the incredible healing possibilities of the rain forest and other areas before it is too late. Thousand of specimens and their chemical constituents and their medicinal potential are being stockpiled before they disappear forever.

One example of a healing plant that is known to many is *Echinacea purpurea*. Echinacea is a wildflower native to the Americas, where Native healers employed it to treat infections, joint pain, abscesses, and dental pain. Echinacea used to be on the National Formulary (or directory of recognized pharmaceutical substances) but was dropped when antibiotics were introduced. Many scientific studies have enumerated the beneficial actions of the remedy, and they include:

- Regeneration of tissue
- Regulation of inflammatory response
- Stimulation of infection-fighting elements such as T cells, phagocytes, lymphocytes, and interferon
- Combating the effects of bacterial "spreading factor," which disrupts human cells

In a health-care setting an extract of the leaves and stems of echinacea is taken orally as a dry, powdered 3.5 percent strength extract (300 mg three times a day), blended in tea or juice, as a remedy for the common cold. It should be avoided by patients with allergies to it or other members of the *Asteraceae* family (marigold, ragweed, daisies, chrysanthemums); by those with autoimmune diseases such as multiple sclerosis, collagen disorders, or rheumatoid arthritis; and by individuals who are taking immune-suppressing drugs.

3

Life Is Not a Race, but It Is a Journey

The road is better than the inn.
—Miguel de Cervantes, *Don Quixote* (Part II, 1615)

Healing is a journey, and every journey needs rules of the road to prevent disasters. The following suggestions will guide your way on the four sacred paths to healing.

First guideline to Native healing: going all natural can be fatal

One misconception many people have about Native healing is that it is all natural. Native Peoples and their healers are eclectic and use the best of both worlds. For example, when the Europeans first brought the strange beasts known as horses to the Americas, it wasn't long before the Indians excelled as riders.

I once met a purist who believed in "all things natural" and who almost killed himself that way. Two years after the Navajo healer experience in the ICU, I volunteered to serve as a refugee-camp doctor in Somalia. Malaria was rampant, and it was camp policy for everyone to take a malaria prevention pill once a week, which was made available to the staff at no cost.

A male co-worker refused. "It's not natural," he said, indicating a preference for personal prayer as protection. He admitted he had not experienced any side effects from the medication, and he understood that the once-weekly pill offered lifesaving prevention.

I suggested that the intravenous quinine we provided our patients who developed cerebral malaria—always fatal unless treated—was originally derived from a natural source, the bark of the cinchona tree. He remained unconvinced. And in spite of all the warnings and assurances, he succumbed to malaria, nearly died, and in the process required round-the-clock nursing and medical care that should have been devoted to the care of the 60,000 desperately ill refugees in our charge.

This story reminds me of the joke, popular among doctors, about a preacher caught in a flood who refuses rescue from helpers in a rowboat and a helicopter, saying to them all, "God will save me." Then he drowns, and in heaven he asks God, "Why didn't you answer my prayer to be saved?" And God answers: "I sent you a rowboat and a helicopter. What more did you want?"

A banana a day will keep the doctor away

On the other hand there are "natural" substances that I advocate for everyone to enjoy regularly. Low potassium can cause you to be 1.5 times more likely to have a stroke, according to a study recently published in the journal *Neurology*. And further research indicated that eating potassium-rich foods such as bananas, leafy green vegetables, avocados, milk, and nuts can dramatically decrease the risk of stroke.

Herbal or natural treatments only?

There are few "purist" Native healers. Most draw on their traditions and on modern medicine as well. Native healers use whatever works. In contrast, many health food stores or alternative medicine practitioners claim they use only natural medicines or herbs. Beware those who promote ceremonies involving peyote (a hallucinogenic cactus) or hallucinogenic mushrooms. You can achieve all the benefits of Native healing without resorting to mind-altering drugs. Be aware, too, that some "pure" natural, herbal remedies when analyzed are found to contain impure components, even dirt.

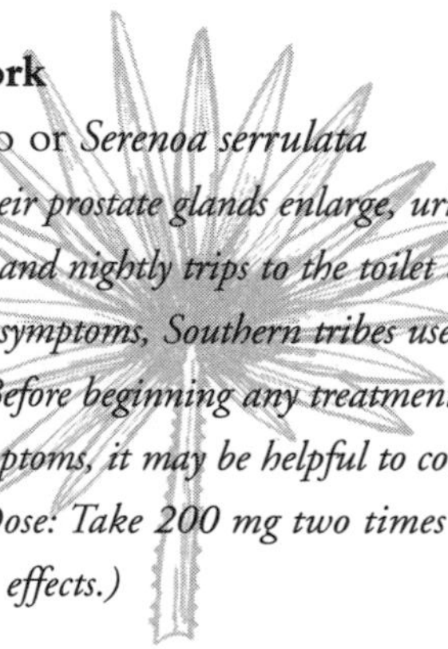

Herbal healing at work

Example: saw palmetto or *Serenoa serrulata*

As adult males age, their prostate glands enlarge, urination becomes more frequent and less forceful, and nightly trips to the toilet become more common. To treat enlarged prostate symptoms, Southern tribes used saw palmetto berries with some success. Note: Before beginning any treatment, see your doctor first. To assess your prostate symptoms, it may be helpful to complete the chart on the following page. (Usual Dose: Take 200 mg two times a day. Usually 3-4 weeks are required to see effects.)

A quick assessment of your prostate symptoms

Regarding urination in the last 4 weeks...

5 = Almost Always 4 = More Than Half the Time 3 = About Half the Time
2 = Less than Half the Time 1 = Less Than 1 Time in 5 0 = Not at All

1. How often have you had the sensation of not emptying your bladder completely after you finished?	5	4	3	2	1	0
2. How often have you had to go again less than 2 hours after you finished?	5	4	3	2	1	0
3. How often have you found you stopped and started again?	5	4	3	2	1	0
4. How often have you found it difficult to postpone going?	5	4	3	2	1	0
5. How often have you had a weak stream?	5	4	3	2	1	0
6. How often have you had to push or strain to begin?	5	4	3	2	1	0
7. How many times did you get up to go at night? (times)	5	4	3	2	1	0

Degree of Severity: Mild (0-7); Moderate (8-19); Severe (20-35)
(Adapted from the American Urological Association survey)

Hormone replacement therapy—what to do?

The Women's Health Initiative (WHI) recently stopped its study of hormone replacement therapy, or HRT, after the discovery that progestin-estrogen hormone replacement could increase the risk of breast cancer, blood clots, stroke, and heart attack. So millions of women have been left wondering what to do about HRT. It's not a simple situation. The popular press described these results as a revelation, but many physicians found the WHI results less than startling for several reasons.

One size doesn't fit all

First, the WHI used hormone replacement therapy that combined progestin (synthetic progesterone) and Premarin (estrogen from the urine of pregnant mares) at dosages that were higher than those required to reduce the symptoms of menopause. In contrast to the standard HRT used by the Women's Health Initiative, many women have relied on compounding pharmacies that *vary* the amount of the hormones needed by each woman during the month according to her *individual* needs.

Actually the risks for progestin-estrogen were less than overwhelming: For 10,000 women there might be eight more strokes, eight breast cancers, and

A brief guide to herbal medications

1/3 of all Americans use them and spend,
on average $150 per year
$5 billion is spent on herbal medications per year
80% of world population uses them
70% of German physicians prescribe them
1/3 of drugs in Germany are herbal/botanicals
25% of all drugs are derived from plants

eight heart attacks. No increase was found for estrogen therapy only (although another study detected an increase in ovarian cancer for ten years of use).

In contrast, the WHI learned that progestin-estrogen users had a lower risk of fractures—and more women die each year from osteoporotic fractures than from ovarian and breast cancer combined. However, many are concluding that the risks of HRT are unacceptable. Others have found that for short term use, particularly in the first five years of menopause, the benefits exceed the hazards. The search for safer alternatives has been underway for some time. Options under review include:

- Maca, a turnip-like plant from the Peruvian Andes, which might be a viable replacement for HRT
- Swiss chard, which may preserve bone density, as can soy and other supplements

In addition, drugs known as bisphosphonates (Fosamax) and SERMS (Selective Estrogen Receptor Modulators), such as raloxifene, can protect bone without estrogen's potential for cancer. Both alternative drugs have side effects and have to be taken without drinking or eating, and while the patient remains standing or upright for half an hour.

One problem is that neither class of drug builds bone; they only preserve what's left. Women need to consider other strategies, including:

- Avoid alcohol, caffeine, cigarettes, salt, and high meat ingestion.
- Eat fruits, vegetables, legumes, and whole grains.
- Consume 2-4 tablespoons of ground flax meal each day.

- Ingest calcium-rich foods:
  women ages 19-49 need 1000 mg/day.
  those ages 50+ need 1000-1500 mg/day.
- Add 400 International Units (IUs) of Vitamin D/day to increase calcium absorption
- Soy, either as tofu, soy nuts, soy beans, or soy milk, can have the benefits of a SERM, but without the side effects of hot flashes.
- Increase physical activity.

Everything physically active helps, though recent research indicates that higher impact choices like jogging, brisk walking, and impact aerobics help more than lower impact activities such as swimming. Unfortunately, high impact can lead to injury to joints and bones. If you prefer higher impact aerobics or jogging, start slow, wear cushioned supportive shoes, run on softer surfaces (grass, a cushioned track, etc.), and avoid these activities altogether if you have musculoskeletal symptoms.

Multivitamins/multimineral supplements

Don't just take calcium. Bone is made up of phosphorus also. Calcium supplements alone will absorb phosphorus and weaken bone, so ensure phosphorus is included in your multivitamin/mineral. Of course osteoporosis was unheard of in traditional societies. Women and men (who comprise 20 percent of osteoporosis victims) were more active and reliant on a diet richer in calcium/phosphorus foods than their descendents are today. Because so few people in industrialized societies consume enough vitamin-filled fruits, vegetables, and nuts, the American Medical Association now recommends a daily multiple vitamin from a respected supplier. In fact, folic acid (a supplement added by the manufacturer) in fortified grains and other foods has already reduced neural tube defects (such as spina bifida) in newborns by half.

Safety

Herbs, vitamins, amino acids, and minerals are classified as dietary or nutritional supplements. They can be sold without proof of safety, quality, or efficacy. The Federal Drug Administration (FDA) has to prove they are unsafe before these medications can be banned. Safer brands, especially high-quality standardized extracts, are becoming available. ConsumerLab.com, an independent testing company, publishes the names of brands that meet minimum quality standards.

What are the risks?

Lacking an FDA guarantee of safety, purity, or efficacy, the consumer of herbal medication must be cautious. Herbal medicines may cause unintended effects. For example, a combination of eight herbs (PC-SPES) intended to improve the male immune system had a strong estrogen effect and caused breast tenderness and blockage of veins (deep vein thrombosis). Foxglove-based digitalis has potent effects on the heart, some of which are toxic. Also toxic are heavy metals such as lead, mercury, and arsenic, which can enter herbs stored or prepared in clay or metal pots. Use medicines from the People's Republic of China with caution. Chinese medicines made in the United States or Taiwan generally meet higher standards. Finally, certain plant products when combined with sunshine produce an intense photodermatitis, or painful redness in areas of the skin exposed to sun.

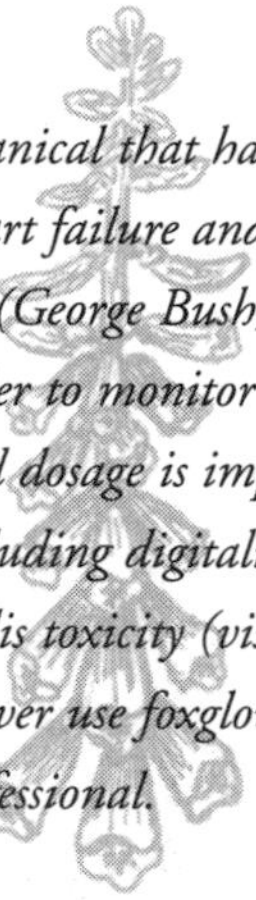

Foxglove or digitalis

Foxglove is a powerful heart botanical that has been used extensively for conditions such as heart failure and the irregular heart rhythm known as atrial fibrillation (George Bush, Sr. suffered from this condition). Overdosage was easier to monitor with the botanical than with the purified digitalis. And dosage is important: When women used a mixture of herbs, including digitalis, for "internal cleansing," they suffered from digitalis toxicity (vision problems, nausea, and heart disturbances). Never use foxglove or digitalis unless prescribed by a licensed medical professional.

Second guideline to Native healing: confidentially speaking

Many voices and healing experiences are part of this book. They are its soul—without which there would be nothing to say. But I have respected the medical confidentiality of patients and healers, and although sources are given throughout this book, a shopping list of healers is not. Native healers are a reticent bunch, reluctant to advertise except by word of mouth, and reluctant to have their sacred ceremonies and activities publicized on film or in other media. For example, video cameras are forbidden at the annual Wa:k Pow-wow of the San Xavier Tohono O'odham, Southern Arizona's largest festival of American Indian dancing, food, and crafts. Legitimate Native healers are the lowest-key, most self-effacing practitioners I have ever encountered. You won't find them in the Yellow Pages or on the covers of grocery store checkout magazines. Fortunately, half of all American Indians live in urban areas, so you won't have far to travel to meet a healer. For information on visiting tribal homelands, contact:

- www.indiannations.visitmt.com
- www.indiancountrytourism.com
- www.Navajo.org

Third guideline to Native healing: contact a local practitioner

This book is designed to offer items of general interest to the reader. It is not intended to address individual problems or to offer medical or legal advice. A local health care practitioner should be consulted for recommendations on any symptoms or medical conditions. The author specifically disclaims any liability, loss, or risk, personal or indirectly from the use and application of any of the contents of this book.

Fourth guideline to Native healing: name-calling

American Indian, Native American, First Nations, Tribal, Native Nations, Native Peoples? Which is appropriate? (When in doubt, always ask.) Each of these terms is used by some people who are the indigenous inhabitants of the Americas and all are used interchangeably throughout this book. For clarity the word "Native" is capitalized when it refers to Native healers and healing, and so is the word "White" when it refers to ethnicity. Healing words derived from Native American languages are defined in the glossary at the back of this book.

Fifth guideline to Native healing: the power of belief

The previous discussion about the coworker who relied on prayer alone to prevent malaria is not intended to deny the power of belief, prayer, or spirituality in the healing process. The intent of this book is to reinforce the effectiveness of this force on healing. Spirituality can also ease the burden when healing is not possible. "May the story give you strength," goes the Indian saying. May the belief relieve your pain.

Native healers are often able to elevate their patients beyond the physical to a higher healing level. Sound kooky, New Age, or superstitious? Consider the following exchange I once had with Joe, a Yakima healer from the Pacific Northwest.

"I can't explain how it works, but it does," Joe told me. And then he did explain, or rather describe, a phenomenon I've heard about from other healers: "I turn the corner with the patient and then we are in the light." As he spoke his eyes had that ten-mile look of someone gazing into an unseeable distance. He went on to say that in that "light" is a vision of well-being where broken hearts and bodies are healed, and where many times the true cause of an illness is found. Once found it is more easily remedied. (For more discussion on going into the light, see Chapters 5, 8, and 9, which consider healing ceremonies, and Chapter13, which discusses the life cycle and death.)

Skeptics and scans

As a physician I found all of this unscientific and unprovable at first, until I learned of the work of A. B. Newberg and E. D'Aquili. Using an imaging technique known as a SPECT scan (SPECT is an acronym for "single-photon emission computed tomography"), these researchers photographically mapped human brains during intense meditation and prayer. SPECT analyzes blood flow—an indicator of brain activity. The left parietal area of the brain is the orientation association (OA) region, which helps us tell the difference between our physical selves and everything else.

SPECT scans of individuals at prayer or in meditation revealed an astonishing confirmation of Native healer Joe's description of turning the corner and going into the light. During these reflective moments blood flow drops significantly to the OA area, and the individual experiences an unlimited connection beyond his or her individual self with the light, or the universe—

a place where the body is not separated from everything else, such as the concept of soul or mind. The spirit does run through the body during these special spiritual times.

Can an extension of our selves through imagery—a belief in something spiritual—have a healing benefit and relieve something as painful as surgery? Yes, answers psychotherapist Peggy Huddleston, M.T.S. She is the author of *Prepare for Surgery, Heal Faster: A Guide of Mind-Body Techniques*, whose techniques were featured on the PBS series *Body and Soul*. Peggy guides patients to visualize their recovery, to use healing statements that reduce pain medication use, and to surround themselves with the love of family and friends.

The tribe or family works because when one member is down, the others can pick him or her up. What we have, including our wealth, is to be shared.
—Adrian, Onondaga elder

Practical value?

By now you're wondering, "How is this going to help me with my next head cold or something worse?" In February of 1997 I had the opportunity to use this visualization technique when I almost died. While I was fixing an irrigation pipe in my yard, an unseen critter bit me on my arm. That small bite sent me to St. Joseph's Hospital in Tucson, Arizona, with an infection unresponsive to oral and intramuscular antibiotics. Within hours, bacteria were taking over my fevered body and I was on intravenous medication. Unfortunately, antibiotic-resistant bacteria are everywhere, increasing in severity, and ready to attack healthy people with good immunity like myself.

PRACTICAL SUGGESTION

I tried a visualization technique. I imagined I was covered with white blood cells (the body's infection fighters) gobbling up bacteria. As these healing cells spread I added an image to the visualization in my mind. I imagined that everything about me, my skin, body, and soon the room where I lay, was covered with light—an easy imaginative extension since white blood cells are light in color. When the nurse interrupted my reverie to resupply my antibiotic drip, I left a "bookmark" in my brain. After she departed I began again where I'd left off.

Can I prove that visualization, a "going into the light" of the type advised by Yakima Joe or Peggy Huddleston, cured me? Would I stop the antibiotics like my coworker in Somalia who contracted malaria because he believed prayer alone would suffice? The answer to both questions is no. Did light imagery refocus my despair of ever recovering and turn it into something more productive? Did it help restore a feeling of personal control? Yes, on both counts. Note: You don't have to know what a white blood cell looks like. Imagine small sponges soaking up disease. A friend suggested the image of a chomping Pac-Man in the video game of the same name.

Do you need a dramatic disease to use visualization? Certainly not. In fact, I recommend its use early, before you become severely ill. Does it replace Western medicine? Don't count on it, but in conjunction with modern care, it just might assist in healing, by acting as an accessory to other processes. Think of a Mayan Indian step pyramid as an example.

The layers at the top of the pyramid are inseparable from the middle and base. Without the strength of each section the structure would tumble. So it is

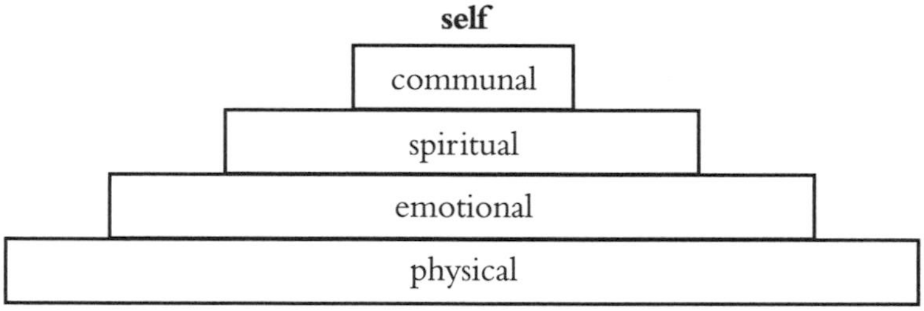

with Native healing. Each separate step or path supports and is integral to the rest of the healing pyramid. Pyramids have been employed by the United States Drug Administration (USDA) to emphasize the essential food groups because the visual image conveys not only the essentials of healthy nutrition, but also its interdependence. Eating all protein—focusing on one food group to the exclusion of others—is unhealthy and leads to stress on the kidneys and liver and a condition called ketosis. In contrast, the malnourished children I worked with in Somalia, who ate a diet of carbohydrates without protein, suffered from an affliction called kwashiorkor, which is often fatal. Each source of nutrition works best in combination with the others.

The USDA food pyramid provides a useful example of the healthy practice of promoting interrelationships that will be explored further in subsequent chapters.

USDA Pyramid and more

I've worked on drastically injured patients in the emergency room, where I started intravenous lines to pump in lifesaving blood and fluids. Visualization won't save anyone in the acute setting. But later it can help you fight a wound infection from the trauma, or provide a useful image of a return to function for an injured limb during rehabilitation.

The USDA pyramid can be extended to include other healthy living components as follows:

- physical activity
- mental activity
- social engagement
- nutrition

Haven't a prayer

First, let's go back for a moment to the huddle of doctors who surrounded the recovered Hosteen, my patient in the intensive care bed on the Navajo Reservation.

"You doctors gave me good care," he said graciously, "but so did the medicine man."

Medicine and healing, body and mind or spirit, have been intertwined ever since prehistoric peoples crushed leaves for a wound poultice and said a healing prayer. Only with the advent of modern technology did these approaches to healing become separate.

Many people believe that the current intense interest in alternative or integrative approaches to health is an attempt to recapture an important synthesis or a holistic approach to medicine that existed in former times. My medical colleagues counter with: "What about practice guidelines?" Practice guidelines are medical "cookbooks" that offer standard tests and treatments for various diseases. However, they were designed for and based on studies of patients who only had one condition and who were generally younger than the average American population. Like any tool they are useful, but not for every situation, patient, or condition. Practice guidelines remind me of the user's guide to my computer. It tells me what to do and not to do, but doesn't offer guidance on how to write or innovate.

BODY

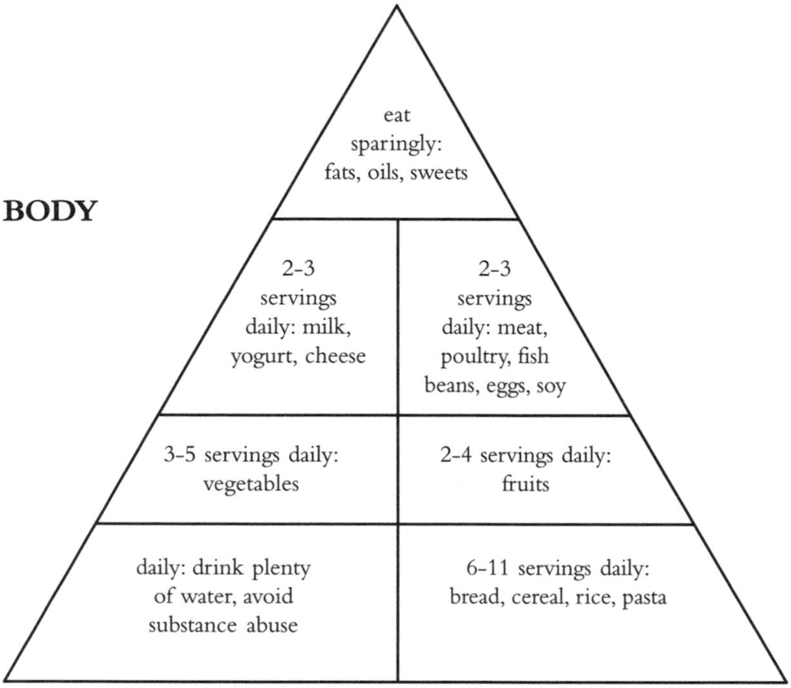

NUTRITION "Eat Right!"

MOTION

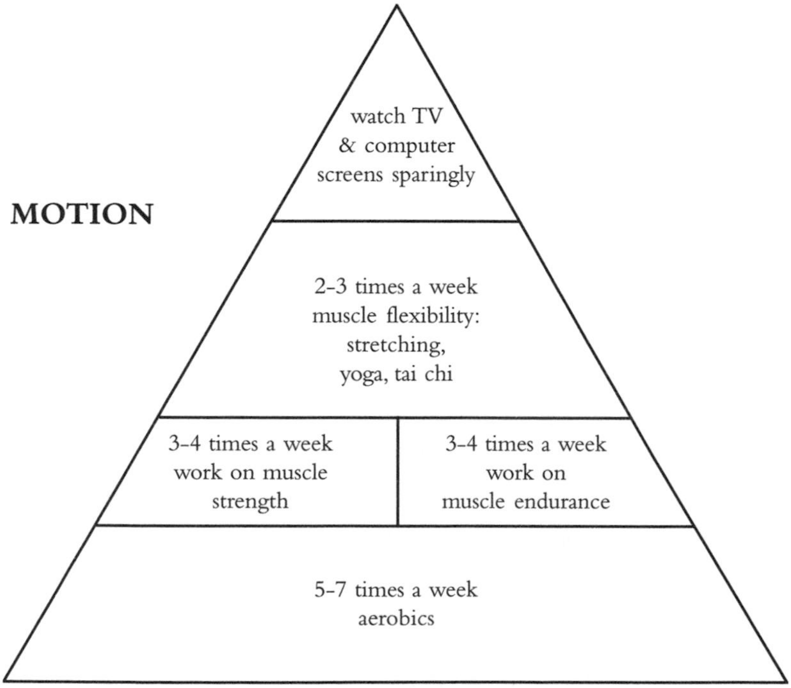

PHYSICAL ACTIVITY "Keep Moving!"

MIND

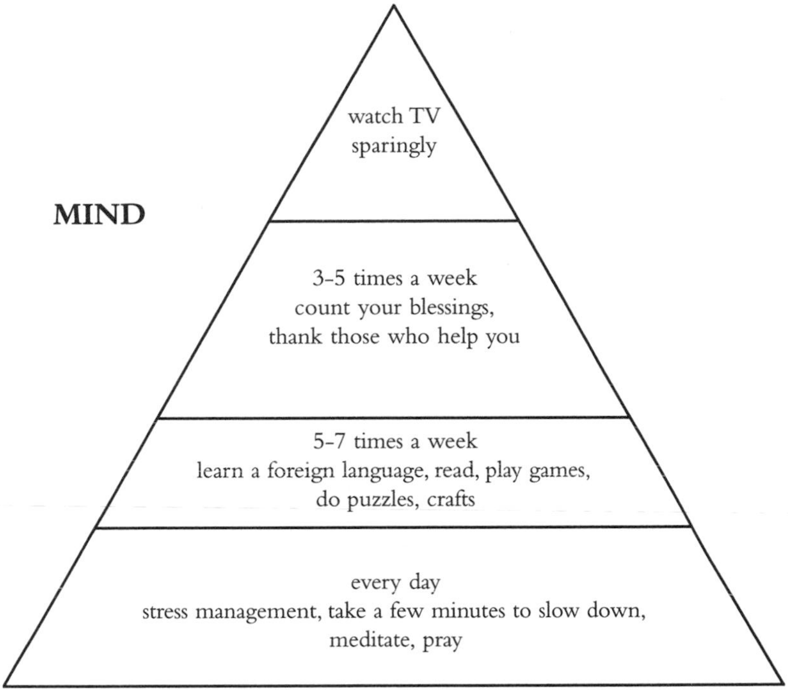

MENTAL ACTIVITY "Engage the Brain!"

SOUL

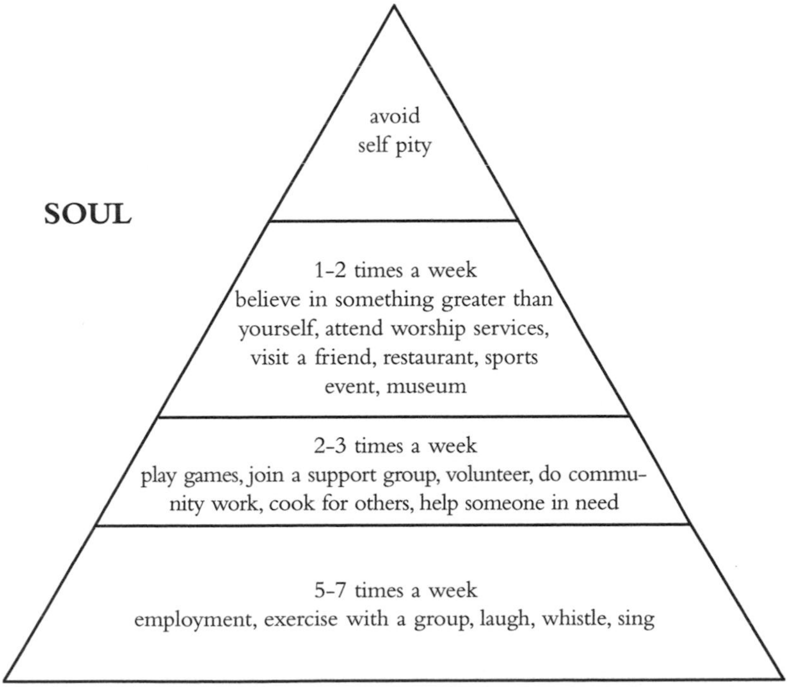

SOCIAL ENGAGEMENT "Get Involved!"

Live twice as long

The average lifespan in the industrialized world has doubled in the past century. Don't vaccines, antibiotics, and surgery take most of the credit? What do the interrelationships between mind and body, medicine and healing, have to do with these dramatic improvements in longevity? The answer, long understood by Native healers, might surprise you.

Resources

Body and Soul series, Public Broadcasting System (January 1999).

Bone density and timing of hormone replacement therapy. J Clin Endocrinol Metab 2001 Dec;86:5700-5.

D'Aquili E, Newberg AB. The mystical mind: probing the biology of religious experience. Minneapolis (MN): Fortress Press;1999.

Fairfield KM, Fletcher RH. Vitamins for chronic disease prevention in adults. JAMA 2002; 287: 3116-3129.

Green DM, Ropper AH, Kronmal RA, Psaty B M, Burke GL. Serum potassium as risk factors for stroke. Neurology 2002; 59: 314-20.

Huddleston , Peggy, M.T.S., Prepare for surgery, heal faster: a guide of mind-body techniques, Cambridge (MA): Angel River Press;1996.

McGinnis JM,Foege WH. The actual causes of death in the United States. JAMA 1993; 270:2207-12.

MRC Vitamin Study Research Group. Prevention of neural tube defects: results of the Medical Research Council Vitamin Study. Lancet 1991; 338: 131-37.

Newberg AB, D'Aquili E, Rause V. Why God won't go away: brain science and the biology of belief. New York: Ballantine;2001.

4

Canoes and Cures: a history

If at first the idea is not absurd then there is no hope for it.
—Albert Einstein (1879-1955)

I remember seeing as a kid a Western movie about two tribes at war. Both sides lined up facing each other, the braves all hungry for killing. A chief from each side rode forward for a final parley before the fight. Suddenly, their determined, fearsome faces softened. They recognized each other from their undergraduate days at Dartmouth College in New Hampshire! The battle was over before it started.

As fictional as the story seemed at the time, Dartmouth College actually was established in 1769 by its founder, the Rev. Eleazar Wheelock, to "civilize" the Indians. While in medical school there, I met Skip, an Oklahoma Cherokee with a special talent. Healing? Canoeing? No, fishing. And more.

Skip is what I call a Renaissance Redman, a Native healer with enormous breadth of knowledge and ability. He paints in oils, fishes, runs a large clinic in Indian country, and has two well-adjusted kids and a delightful wife. Most of all, the spirit runs through everything he says or does.

Not a large person physically, but enormous in character and heart, Skip has the quiet demeanor of his Native forebears and their tenacity as well. How so? He never gives up on a patient. Skip lives the four pathways plus. He can always create a new opportunity for change for the better. He represents the best of the integrative approach to medicine proposed by Dr. Andrew Weil and others, *and* he includes the patient's family, community, and spirituality in the process of healing.

At Dartmouth Medical School Skip used to rescue me from the drudgery of study and take me out on his canoe on the Connecticut River. I'm not a fisherman by desire or background, but the change was therapeutic. Even more so was my interaction with Skip, a Native healer in training at Dartmouth Medical School. I learned a lot about Native healing while paddling a canoe with him.

From Skip I learned about our connection with nature, which heretofore in my case had been largely as a consumer—if it moos or clucks or swims, I'd eat it. Skip wanted me to catch fish, but with more than a hook, with a soul. Sound goofy?

I would reel in my fish, and he would examine them and release half of them. "Too young ... this one isn't ready yet ... this one is a mom filled with roe (eggs)," he would say. The "keepers" received a blessing of thanks for giving their lives that we might eat. And eat them we did at Skip's place, usually joined by other starving, impoverished students like us. Fishing was more than a sport; it was vital calories.

But something changed in me. Holding an animal in my hands, repeating Skip's prayer of thanks to it for giving its life that I might live, and then cutting its head off before I ate it made me ponder. Nourishment was no longer a plastic-wrapped frozen product at the meat counter of the local grocery store.

It made me ponder about something worse. We did unnecessary experiments on animals in medical school. One professor wanted to show medical students the effects of a fatal allergic reaction (or anaphylaxis), so each student was given a guinea pig to inject with a substance, and then we were instructed to record its death throes. Not only was this a cruel way to die, but it was wasteful of life and money. Raising sixty-five guinea pigs to maturity each year isn't cheap (I know, I feed one at our home). The larger message was, "We humans rule and we can take life whenever we want."

Mind you, this was not ground-breaking research using animals to uncover the cure for a dread disease. It was purely and simply animal cruelty. After hearing dissent from more senior students, the faculty voted to kill only one animal for every four students, and later, more sensibly, to videotape the event so that no further deaths occurred. On another occasion, for our final, the same department had us kill several animals to show the effects of other drugs. Again, the research was done. We were only repeating what was known and published in our textbooks. A group of us asked if we could show our knowledge of drug effects with a written or oral exam. Weathering considerable resentment against uppity students who should know their place, a small number of us were allowed to take an oral exam, far more difficult than injecting a lab rat under the skin and recording the effects. For years afterward, the secretary for that department would greet me coldly with, "So you're the one who wants us to do research on humans instead of animals!"

I replied that new research on unsolved problems warranted using animals, but that repeating an experiment that had been solved for years, and unnecessarily killing a living being in the process, was not. But my words fell on unhearing ears. She was only repeating what the faculty (who should have been able to tell the difference between those two points of view) had told her in anger. Weren't doctors supposed to preserve life when possible, not take it? Some years later I chose to not eat animals, though I respect those who still do, especially one like Skip who honors what he has received from another creature.

What was Skip's religion, I wondered. He explained that there were many variations, just as there were in Christianity and other faiths (I'm still trying to sort out all the different types of Baptist denominations I encountered in North Carolina). Some Native Americans like the Apache are strictly monotheists like Muslims or Jews or Unitarian Christians. Others believe in the many faces of God like Trinitarian Christians and Hindus. What is central to all is a respect for life, nature, community, and preservation of the Earth's bounty for years to come. "Let that fish go; she is full of eggs," captured it for Skip. Think of the effects of your actions on the next generation. Skip, like many Native people, incorporated indigenous practices into Christianity or the "Jesus Way." This meld is stronger among indigenous groups in Latin America where assimilation into European ways is less pronounced.

God's Way?

You called us savages when we prayed to God,
Because you said your God was one of peace and forgiveness,
And then you put your cavalry sword through our children when they begged for mercy at Wounded Knee and Fort Grant.
You made my children learn about the Saviour feeding the loaves and fishes to the poor,
And killed all of our Pite (buffalo) and moved us to bad lands that would not grow food.
We gave "unto Caesar that which is Caesar's" and gave you our best lands.
We shared what food we had at the first Thanksgiving.
We turned the other cheek time and again.
We forgave you seven times seven.
Who is the savage?

—Iroquois healer

5

How to Double Your Lifespan

Men dig their Graves with their own Teeth and die more by those fated Instruments than by the Weapons of their Enemies.
—Thomas Moffett, M.D.,
Health's Improvement (1655)

The White man talks about the mind and body and spirit as if they are separate. For us they are one. Our whole life is spiritual from the time we get up until we go to bed.
—Joe, Yakima healer

The average lifespan in the industrialized world has doubled in the past century. Every year, as part of a class I teach, I ask a group of medical students to tell me why this is true. They usually give vaccines, antibiotics, and surgery most of the credit. But what is the real answer? Think about tuberculosis—the great killer known as the white plague in my grandparents' time. Examine the graph on the following page.

Deaths from tuberculosis dropped drastically long before modern medicine produced a cure. Change the disease to measles, and the decline is the same. This is also true for whooping cough and other diseases that devastated our relatives. (My wife's great-grandparents lost three children to diphtheria in one week.)

So, if it wasn't antibiotics or vaccines or modern medical care, what is the reason for the doubling of life expectancy? Improved standard of living, less crowding, sanitation, community relationships, public health nurses, or a combination of these? Can non-physical factors that have nothing to do with doctors or hospitals or medicines improve health? The answer is a resounding yes.

"The greatest contribution to decreased cardiovascular disease in our study in Massachusetts wasn't hospital cardiac cure units, it was changes in lifestyle," said James Dalen, M.D., past dean of the College of Medicine at the University of Arizona, and editor of the journal *Archives of Internal Medicine*. How can this be true?

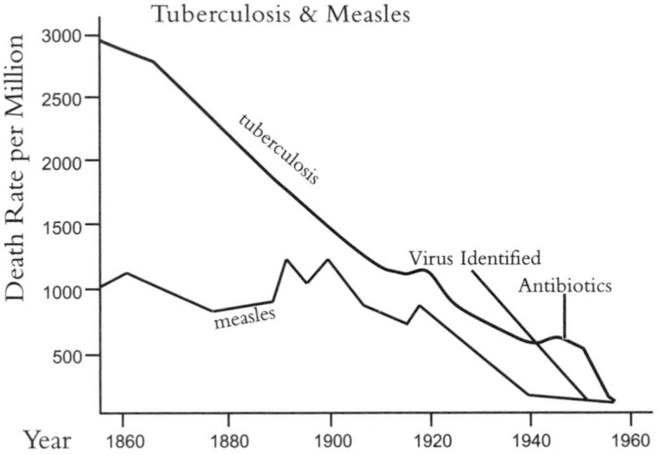

Non-medical factors and health

When I was in medical school, spirituality was not part of the curriculum—a significant void, considering the conclusions of research on its powerful effects on health. For example, regular participants in worship services increase their longevity by seven years. In fact, religious participation is so powerful that it counterbalances the negative effects of smoking! Similar studies have found that religious participation leads to improvements in relaxation response, blood pressure, heart performance, and mental health. In addition, Duke University conducted a study of almost 4,000 older adults and found that worship decreases depression and anxiety.

What's going on? What does this have to do with Native healing and wak'a—the spirit that runs through the body—and the other three sacred pathways?

Distress or stress?

Consider the physical effects of stress, a mental condition we all encounter. Stress can produce excess hormones in the body, elevate blood pressure leading to stroke, and diminish immunity, which can predispose to infections. A supportive community, family, traditions, healing or other ceremonies, friends, and members of a congregation all seem to provide a circle of protection against life's ills, including the stress of isolation, loneliness, poorly-balanced priorities, and overextended living. Native healers were not surprised by these findings, having understood the benefits of community since the beginning.

Iron men and women

Sometimes modernity creates disease. Traditionally, Native Peoples and others, including our ancestors, cooked in iron utensils whose use added essential iron to their diet and helped prevent anemia. Modern salespeople convinced them to buy shiny aluminum pans, and iron-deficiency anemia started to rise.

Fortunately, many edible plants are iron-rich, such as curly dock or Ramex crispus. *Pick the younger leaves at the top, boil until the leaves are limp, and serve. I add vinegar. Avoid plants by a roadside that might have been sprayed with herbicide, automobile fuels, oils, or lubricants.*

PRACTICAL SUGGESTION: Create a personal sanctuary

Try creating a personal sanctuary to focus your thoughts on what is truly valuable, eternal, or spiritual. A good rule of thumb: Focus on the eulogy—what you stand for, believe in, feel closest to, not the obituary—where you lived, went to school, worked, etc. Each day observe one thing you find heartwarming, funny, encouraging, or lovely. Our staff collects cartoons, positive stories, photos, and thank-you cards from patients, and shares them. Every day these objects of beauty (or hozho in Navajo) boost our spirits.

Joy, not happiness

A successful industrialist on his deathbed shared this thought with me: "What really matters to me now isn't my bank account or my big house … it's my family and my friends. Remember that and you'll have a joyful life."

I thought it was curious that he said joyful, not happy. I now understand the difference. No one can ever be happy all the time. Who is happy to hear that a close friend has died unexpectedly? Most, however, on reflection are joyful about the opportunity to have known that person, to have shared moments, hopes, and dreams.

My patient especially liked this quote from a rabbinical sage: "Who is rich? He who finds joy in what he has."

Unless you are especially gifted at keeping the enduring and non-superficial in mind, you may require a reminder. Another patient told me he likes to watch his son sleep each night as a reminder of the important things in life, and the joy of it, and as a way of restoring balance to his life. Native healers often provide those seeking help with something they can see and hold as a reminder and as a symbol of healing.

As one healer commented to me, "The Whites say life is a rat race. If you believe that, then all you see and think about all day long are rats."

How does one disconnect from a world of stress and commercialism? Could a personal focus on the spiritual in my life have any healing value? (I almost wrote "spiritual side," suggesting a separation of this element from the rest of me, and then I remembered Yakima Joe's admonition that all life is spiritual.) First I had to ask myself, "What do you have?" Then over some months I collected symbols of what I valued, including:

- A tool my deceased dad owned, a remembrance of an immigrant who survived the tragedy of five years of Nazi bombing—a representation that hope is eternal.
- A pink ribbon to remind me of a relative with breast cancer—a reminder that when you have health you have everything.
- A photo of my family—whose love nourishes my soul.
- A shard of 900-year-old Hohokam Indian pottery that I found on our homestead—a remembrance that others lived here before us and that we should honor the past.
- A piece of the Berlin Wall—a reminder that freedom is fragile but never truly dies.

Once a day I look at the corner where I keep my personal sanctuary. Sometimes I look for minutes, oftentimes less. Lately, I gaze at that pink ribbon to remind me of my relative's healing journey to become not a cancer victim, but a person who happens to have cancer, a journey that was assisted by a community support group. Breast cancer support groups, by the way, were not started by cancer surgeons but by women who banded together to help each other navigate the frightening world of chemotherapy, radiation, and surgical disfigurement. Such support groups may not cure, but they have been shown to reduce pain and suffering.

PRACTICAL SUGGESTION

How long will you be dead? Sometimes it is hard to achieve any sense of transcendence. Our lives are so swamped with humdrum day-to-day concerns that it is hard to turn the mind's motor off and reflect on what is truly important to us. One technique that helps focus thoughts on the long-lasting instead of the trivial things is to write the epitaph for your own headstone, or, if you plan on cremation, a memorial plaque. If someone with whom I'm working is up to it, I ask my patient to write his or her obituary, and then a eulogy—what others might say about them. Some are amusing, others heart-wrenching. Try yours now.

Name:
Born:
Place(s) Lived:
Family:
Proudest Accomplishment:
Final Words:

Were you surprised at your answers, or at the difficulty in setting enduring priorities? After completing this form, one person told me, "I'm a consultant and I help companies write their mission statements—what they stand for. I realized I had never thought about what I stood for. No wonder I'm stressed out. I'm racing around chasing the wrong things!"

The importance of ceremony

Oftentimes, ceremonies restore a healthy balance. We are all familiar with life ceremonies such as a wedding, a funeral, a confirmation, a bar or bat mitzvah. Even modern rites of passage such as getting a driver's license might count. But is that all there is to it? What do Native healers mean by "ceremony"?

The ceremony of healing

"Ceremonies are so a person may speak from the heart and know his thoughts are respected," said Joe, the Yakima healer. "I have a bright light I enter when I do a healing ceremony. In the scientific world you go from A to B. When I perform a ceremony the light goes up and down, sideways and all around."

What is this light? "It is a gift given in the spirit," he explained. "There is no money that can buy it—you just go through it from two years old till the day you decide to go [die]. When medicine men are ready to go, they go. They aren't sick—they just decide they've done what they want to do."

He described the healer's experience in the healing ceremony: "Once you go into a ceremony you go into the light, around the curve, and you bring them [patients] back from another world where they are already dead [from lack of spirituality]."

Spirituality underlies everything, from the beginning to the end of the experience. "Spirituality is not just one part of our life, it *is* our life, from the time we get up to the time we go to sleep," said Yakima Joe.

Is this focus on spirituality and ceremony bogus, compared to science? Does anyone benefit, or is it a waste of limited health resources? Thomas Morse, M.D., outlined for me the benefits of a Vietnam veterans study, in which Indians with conditions that are related to military service are referred by modern medical providers to Native healers for traditional ceremonies. Of the 200 known Navajo ceremonies, twelve have been authorized (including the Enemy Way and the Beauty Way) by the Veterans Administration for their healing benefits. These ceremonies range from one hour to ten days in length, and they cost from $50 to $750. They have proven particularly effective with PTSS (post-traumatic stress syndrome), and appear to successfully bridge a gap between Western and traditional approaches. Participants describe a restoration of healing balance as a result of the ceremonies. Afterward, many are able to discontinue all medication.

Spiritually-based ceremonies appear to have a powerful health effect on American Indians. What about other people?

Spiritual healers

Well-respected, mainstream physicians also advocate a spiritual approach to medicine. One such physician is Joseph E. Murray, M.D., a Nobel Prize winner, organ transplant leader, and professor emeritus at Harvard Medical School. In his autobiography, *Surgery of the Soul: Reflections on a Curious*

Career, Murray argued that patients are more than symptoms: They are people with a spirit. If the spiritual side is nurtured, he suggested, they can be helped most effectively through modern medicine. "Work is a prayer, and I start off every morning dedicating it to our Creator ... every day is a prayer—I feel that, and I feel that very strongly," wrote Murray. He is not a televangelist faith-healer, but an internationally recognized scientist who advocates a broader medical method that combines the scientific and the spiritual, the modern and the traditional.

Native healing approaches can be integrative, unifying scientific and other methods. Like Western medicine, Native healers collect symptoms, conduct exams, make a diagnosis, and treat patients. Modern physicians use inductive reasoning to gather facts and then make conclusions. Native bone setters and midwives mostly closely follow this Western paradigm. My mom was delivered by a midwife at the family farm in the Mohawk River Valley of New York. What distinguishes the two systems is the fact that Native healing does not make the diagnosis the person. When I was an intern, more experienced physicians would often tell me to "go see the gallbladder in room 212," rather than personalizing the request with the individual's name. And I would leave, feeling that to my would-be mentors the individual had become the disease.

Parallels: Native healing and western medicine

Both traditions:

Identify a chief complaint	*Take a history*
Conduct a physical exam	*Make a diagnosis*
Give an assessment	*Carry out a plan*
Provide treatment	*Offer aftercare*

The I-am-not-a-headache ceremony

Two remarkable things tend to occur once you decide that, even though you have a disease, you are not a diagnosis—fibromyalgia or depression or whatever—but a person with a chemical imbalance, or disrupted spirit. Many times this decision makes you feel better. And sometimes you also find the cause of the disease.

Consider the example of my patient with vise-like headaches who was undergoing a divorce.

"I'm spending ninety percent of my time agonizing over why she left me for someone else and ten percent doing my job," Jack said.

All of Jack's diagnostic studies to find a physical reason for his headaches, including a CAT (computerized axial tomography) scan of the head, were normal. Obviously his "ex" was consuming his mind, time, and energy. His all-consuming thoughts about her had staked out space in his brain, and they were making him sick. A Native healing "cleansing" ceremony can provide help for painful unresolved issues such as these that lead to illness.

PRACTICAL SUGGESTION

I told Jack to write a letter and:

- List hurts and pains.
- List any positives coming from the pain. This is not as tough as it sounds. In his case he had two wonderful children from the marriage and the opportunity to enjoy them because the judge gave him primary custody.
- Write down what may have made the other person behave the way he or she did. In Jack's case he had difficulty completing tasks and keeping promises—habits he gradually changed for the better.
- Write down how he thought his mind was punishing him with worry and anger.
- Burn the letter and scatter the ashes in the wind, which he did.

NOTE: Follow all fire safety precautions (fireproof container, wet ashes, etc.) to avoid adding "started wildfire" to your list of hurts and pains.

Jack's headaches resolved, though he asked a critical question: Did this ceremony mean all was forgiven? The answer is that there are many steps to resolution. In Jack's case he had to move on; his anger against his ex-wife was only hurting himself. Is this forgiveness? Not exactly. Full forgiveness requires asking the person you have injured for forgiveness, making restitution, and then not committing the act again.

Medical research supports this approach. The National Institute for Health Care Research at Virginia Commonwealth University in Richmond completed a study that found that when adults think about being wronged, their pulse and blood pressure rates elevate and their moods darken, but the opposite occurs for individuals whose thoughts center on forgiveness. Surely this was true in Jack's case.

I fought the physical and the physical won

Are Nobel laureate Murray and Native healers exaggerating when they emphasize the importance of non-physical ailments and healing conditions? Let's see what we've been taught about the physical side of health. Turn on television and you'll hear:

"The pain reliever doctors recommend most …"

"If you have a pain or symptom you can eliminate it with …"

"Takes fever away fast …"

"Stops diarrhea quickly and effectively …"

"Gets swelling down …"

Painful purpose?

Yes, television is right. We can stop pain, reduce fever, block diarrhea, and reduce swelling. Yet all these symptoms serve a purpose.

Pain sends a message to the body to stop walking on a sprained ankle and rest it so it can heal.

Heat kills germs; this is why dishwashers use hot water. So does fever—the body's own internal heat treatment against disease-carrying pathogens.

Diarrhea occurs when the intestines flush out toxins from contaminated food. In some cases antibiotics can even prolong the carrier state of diarrheal conditions such as salmonella.

Swelling in the ankle serves as a splint to reduce movement and accelerate healing.

Make no mistake. Neuropathic pain (pain that serves no protective purpose), extreme fever that causes seizures, bloody or excessive diarrhea that brings on dehydration and anemia, and pathologic swelling that leads to blood vessel and nerve entrapment are all dangerous. Most cases involving ordinary pain, fever, diarrhea, and swelling are not so serious, fortunately.

And some "modern" treatments, such as ephedrine for nasal congestion, are even dangerous and can lead to fatal abnormal heart rhythms.

You have everything you need

What is essential? The spirit can help you adjust to these bodily changes, according to Dr. Murray and Joe, the Yakima healer. The inner you can trust these symptoms and the messages they are sending you (stop walking on a painful swollen ankle, or don't eat food that has been left out too long). Or you can struggle against these body "communications" and suffer the consequences, such as a crippling injury or other illness.

The solutions are always inside you. The key to Native healers' practice, and the approach that Murray also advocates, is to:

- Tap into the whole of the person's mind, body and spirit—which is greater than the sum of the parts.
- Use all available tools and helpers to assist your own healing of swelling, pain, fever, or whatever symptom your nervous system transmits to you.
- Recognize that of all the above are pathways to the spirit inside you—your unlimited healing potential.

Here is one example of how to recruit an inner capacity to ease a physical burden.

Golden Rule

The best healers follow the original golden rule: Treat your neighbor as you would want to be treated yourself (Leviticus 19:18). Or as one Native healer said to me: "This treatment is what I would do for my mom." That's my measure of caring and quality.

Something not taught in medical school

As an intern I once had to give a gravely ill elderly woman bad news about her lab tests. Her family had left for the day. It was just the two of us. She was elderly, Hispanic, and mostly-Spanish speaking. I was young, mostly White, and limited-Spanish speaking.

"I have disappointing news," I said. "The bone scan shows your cancer is back. It has spread to your bones and brain, and that's why you have bad headaches."

"I thought so," she responded.

"I'm sorry things didn't turn out the way we hoped," I said.

My experience is that many people already suspect the results of their tests. She continued with considerable calm.

"How much time do I have?"

I've found so many cases where the doctor says, "You have six months to live," and the person survives another thirty years, that I only give averages. I answered: "Others have lived three to six months. It can be hard to predict."

"Will I have more pain?" Her soft brown almond eyes met mine with an intensity that reached deep inside me.

"We can help control it with painkillers ... to the very end."

"I guess I won't have to worry about getting hooked on drugs!" She laughed, an inclusive laugh that gave me permission to join her. I did. The tension seemed to lift from the room. I felt a kinship with her and thought, "I hope I am this brave and serene when my time comes."

She seemed to search for words, and then asked, "Would you say a prayer for me?"

"Yes ... I will." I was surprised at my answer, but I felt I was abandoning her if I refused. I wasn't sure what to do next. Was it allowed? I gulped, plunged into unknown medical territory, and asked, "Do you want one now?" She did.

What would Hippocrates say? His oath for doctors demands *primum non nocere*: First do no harm. Did I twist her intravenous-punctured arm to join my faith or to pray? No. She asked me for a prayer, not the reverse. Did I try to convert her? No. Did she find some comfort when I did pray with her? Yes, and she thanked me. I thought back to the Navajo healer who advised me to listen, not to prove I was right. He had helped me treat this dying woman who asked for something I hadn't been taught in medical school—a house of healers who left this enormous question out of the final exam.

Dying for reasons that weren't medical

I learned from her and others that people die for reasons that aren't medical, and they also recover from disease through methods that often aren't related to medicines or surgery.

"But I don't live where I can meet a Native healer or collect herbs or leaves," one friend objected.

"You're lucky. You don't have to rake the leaves up," I said.

All you need is inside your own head. You can create a personal vision of well-being by following healing paths. The next chapters will cover these pathways to healing as practiced by Native Peoples.

Resources

Barry MH, Fowler FJ, O'Leary MP, et al. The American Urological Association symptom index for benign prostatic hyperplasica. J Urol 1992; 148:1549-1557.

Burhansstipanov L, Gilbert A, La Marca K, Krebs LU. An innovative path to improving cancer care in Indian country. Public Health Rep. 2001; 116;424-33.

Chin J, ed. Control of Communicable Diseases Manual. APHA, 2000. Washington DC.

Dalen, J. Lecture on health care in the U.S., Sept 1999, Tucson, AZ.

Feigin R, Greenberg A, Ras H, Hardan Y, Rizel S, Ben Efraim T, Stemmer SM. The psychosocial experience of women treated for breast cancer by high dose chemotherapy supported by autologous stem cell transplant: a qualitative analysis of support groups. Psychooncology. 2000;9;57-68.

Goodwin P et al. The effect of group psychosocial support in metastatic breast cancer. New England J Med 2001; 345:1719-26, 1767-8.

Kelly K. Breast cancer support groups. Do they affect survival? Lancet. 1998; 55;32-3.

Maunsell E, Brisson J, Deschenes L. Social support and survival among women with breast cancer. Cancer. 1995;76;631-7.

Murray J. Surgery of the soul: reflections on a curious career. Canton (MA): Science History Publications;2001.

6

A Card-Carrying Optimist: a history

We are not disturbed by things but rather by the view that we take of them. When we meet with troubles let us never blame anyone but rather our opinion about things.

—Epictetus (c. 60 A.D.)

Kermit was a teenaged boy sent to Arizona to die. He had contracted tuberculosis in the early 1940s back home in the Tennessee mountains. Before antibiotics were available the only "treatment" for his disease—also known as the white plague because it killed millions each year—was plenty of sunshine.

While his friends were attending high school, courting sweethearts, and saving for college, Kermit found himself in a tuberculosis hospital ward with twenty other diseased men, a cheerless fellowship of the nearly dead. Before his illness he had been an accomplished student, especially in mathematics. Here there were no courses or teachers to challenge his maturing mind. There was only a large hospital library, which he refused to visit. "Why bother with books if you're a dead man?" he thought.

He felt desperate in a hospital with nothing to do but cough, hope for a nonexistent cure, and overhear another person's last prayers. His personal plea was for an evening's sleep without the dreadful night sweats of tuberculosis. One morning just before dawn he awoke drenched with perspiration. "God save me or kill me ... I'm ready right now!" he cried into the lingering darkness. A tuberculosis-ridden English teacher in the next bed countered with, "'All things are ready, if our minds be so.' "

"Who said that?" Kermit asked.

"Shakespeare's King Henry the Fifth when he was outnumbered five to one at the battle of Agincourt."

"He died of course."

"Only his fear of trying died. Henry won the field and the crown of France that day."

"I'd like to win a one-way ticket out of this hospital."

"In life you punch your own ticket," answered his roommate.

Kermit mulled over these challenging words. "All things are ready, if our minds be so." The sentence contained two parts. First: "All things are ready." He was certainly ready to leave the hospital, even though he knew he couldn't. The second half of the passage was the most perplexing: "If our minds be so." Making up his mind wouldn't cause his tuberculosis to disappear. In fact, he had hardly used his mind at all since his melancholy arrival in Arizona months before. He realized that despair had dulled his intellect as thoroughly as tuberculosis had invaded his lungs. He had always been good at math. He decided it was time to get back into practice. Why not classify each of his fellow patients according to how "ready," or positive and committed to their own healing they were, and then calculate their odds of survival?

He categorized each patient as an optimist or a pessimist. During the following months he discovered that all of the pessimists died of their tuberculosis. A few of the optimists also died, but their odds of survival were far better. From that moment Kermit decided to become a "card-carrying optimist." His next decision was to stop being a tuberculosis victim and to become a tuberculosis scholar. He went to the library and read everything in print about his affliction. While he was there he stumbled onto other subjects: the humanities, philosophy, and religion. Each new volume became a magic flying carpet of self-deliverance. All he had to do was open a book and away he soared from his prison of illness.

Life for Kermit became an adventure to live for, and to live through. When his doctors wanted to treat his tuberculosis by collapsing his lungs, he refused. He had read an article saying that the procedure was controversial and not as effective as a new and experimental class of drugs called "antibiotics." And eventually when the antibiotic streptomycin became available his mind was ready and his body willing to embark on a journey of five hundred deep and painful injections, one every six hours for three very long months. And Kermit recovered.

Kermit also learned that his fellow optimists were the world's best tutors. The English teacher who had quoted Shakespeare taught him the love of language, reading, and writing. An accountant two beds over coached him in math. A scientist in a neighboring ward instructed him in the wonders of the physical world. While his buddies back home struggled with swollen classes and overburdened teachers, he thrived on the attentions of three personal professors. And he continued his library visits.

Kermit's most remarkable discovery was this: As soon as he committed himself to navigating his body back to healing, something unexpected happened. He set loose a chain of circumstances that led to his eventual recovery. What is more important, he had enrolled himself in his own College of Life-Long Learning, a self-study program that guided and sustained him until his death, forty-eight years after he was sent to Arizona to die!

I met Kermit many years later because he was my accountant, as well as being a pillar of the local community. He intrigued me, partly because entirely on his own Kermit had learned the answer to the same question that Laura Kubzansky, assistant professor of health and social behavior at the Harvard School of Public Health, answered in her study of 2,280 men: Optimists are half as likely to die of heart disease as pessimists. And maybe they are more likely to survive other dangers too. In Shakespeare's play *Henry V* the full exchange runs like this:

King Henry V: All things are ready, if our minds be so.
Westmoreland: Perish the man whose mind is backward now!
(IV.3.77-78)

Optimists have minds whose energy moves them forward to a better place. Punch Woods, President and CEO of one of America's most successful food banks, sums up the optimists' creed: "It's not a question of no or yes, but of how."

Words are powerful. Groups working together to fulfill words are even more powerful. Anyone who has witnessed a Diné (Navajo) sing will recognize the enormous effect of inner and collective healing on the individual. When one member of the clan is ill, others may be recruited to a group chant led by a healer, such as this passage from the Beauty Way ceremony.

Joyful I journey.
Joyful with life-bringing rain clouds I journey.
Joyful with refreshing rain I journey.
Joyful with growing plants, I journey.
Joyful on the pollen trail I journey.
Joyful I journey.

As it was long ago I journey.
Let there be beauty before me.
Let there be beauty behind me
Let there be beauty below me
Let there be beauty all around me.
In beauty it is complete.
In beauty it is complete.

7

North: the first pathway

The spirit runs through the body — spirituality and healing

The greatest discovery of my generation is that human beings can alter their lives by altering their attitudes of mind.
—William James (1842-1910)

After reading this section or pathway you will understand

1. How Native healers and their practices:
   - Heal a broken spirit
   - Create a personal vision of well-being
   - Find and remedy the true cause of illness
   - Develop healing partnerships
2. How to use practical suggestions and personal healing habits to maximize healing in your own life.

What's going on in your life?

Charlie was a well-respected machinist with a minor back injury who wouldn't return to work after weeks of treatment, even though everything—tests, exams, studies—was normal.

Finally, after one of many frustrating, unproductive visits, I asked him, "What's going on in your life?"

He sighed and said, "My wife has a two-hundred-dollar-a-day cocaine habit . . . she sells our stuff, furniture, whatever we own while I'm at work to support her habit. I can't go back to work, or I'll have an empty house."

	NORTH	EAST	WEST	SOUTH
	Sun Duality of light (wave & particle) and humans	Wind Sacredness of words	Rain Life-giving	Earth
ACTION	*Know* Spirit runs through the body	*Understand* Power of relationships	*Build* Healing partnerships	*Create* Harmony with life cycle space/place
DESCRIPTION	Holistic approach Humans are more than a list of physical complaints	Group therapy Group support *No man is an island.*	Doctor-patient relationship Patient-centered care	Self actualization Homeostasis
NATIVE WORDS	Wak'a Care for/treat the soul	Talking stick, Talking circle Words of all heard with respect	Katsinam Convey individual comments/prayers to gods	Hozho Place of beauty (inner harmony)
ICON	Sun	Sweat lodge	Katsina	Sand painting
PATIENT ENCOUNTER	Doctor listens at a deeper level	Understands context of patient's family and community	Patient is center of healing, not to *do* to, but to heal *with*	Convert illness to harmony
EXAMPLE	Male with low back pain, won't go to work. Tests normal.	Wife with cocaine habit. He must stay home.	He could have gone to work, lost wife. Instead she joins Cocaine Anonymous.	He joins co-dependent group. He returns to work.
THERAPEUTICS	Discover true cause of illness	Engage family and co-workers	Develop synergy with patient	Restore natural life cycle

Was Charlie's original injury a fake to get out of work? Actually not. He had a real injury. I felt the muscle spasm. Did the Navajo shaman who visited my ICU patient with deadly high blood pressure succeed because his chant, cornmeal, and cultural understanding cured a psychosomatic or imaginary condition? No, we had objective evidence of a serious elevation of blood pressure.

North: the spirit runs through the body

A person or patient is more than nerves, muscles, tendons, organs—he or she is a will, a soul, a spirit. In the emergency room, immediate action is needed to stop the bleeding. But the best doctors and Native healers listen at a deeper level. My patient just wouldn't get better; he wouldn't even return to the lightest of work duty. Finally I asked and listened at a deeper level. The external Charlie was a mess; the internal Charlie held the answer and the solution. Charlie's wife got treatment after we arranged for help. He returned shortly thereafter to life as a productive breadwinner and a top-notch employee again.

Teacher-learner

Doctor in Latin means teacher, and a teacher implies a learner. The patient is also a teacher because the doctor is always learning from the patient. (A Latin maxim says it another way: *Qui docet discit*, or "he who teaches, learns.") Gaining insight from experience is critical to any doctor's learning (this is why friends tease me that I'm practicing medicine, until I get it right).

Speaking of patients as teachers, and doctors learning from patients, here's my favorite story on this theme. A critically ill patient suffering from a gunshot wound was wheeled into the emergency room. He was losing blood fast, and the odds were against him. A sense of fatalism filled the trauma room. A nurse asked the dying patient, "Are you allergic to anything?" His answer broke the tension: "Yes …" he gasped. "Bullets!" He lifted the spirits of the trauma team, and he survived his emergency surgery. His humorous, spirited response has been retold time and again, often in other cases when undue pessimism and its negative effects on the medical team are banished by the retelling of his story. Humor heals!

North spirit

The spirit runs through the body. For a moment imagine that everything in your life is sacred: the food you eat, the air you breathe, family members, a new dawn, a setting sun. As the Hebrew Scriptures say, *Tzelem Elohim*—humans are made in the sacred image of God (Genesis 9:6). Each human possesses the sacred, the spiritual essence. For traditional Native Americans all things are spiritual from the time they get up until they go to sleep. When the spirit is disturbed, illness can result. Consider the following illustration.

Modernitis: a Native healing story

One day in our clinic a young woman named Beth came unglued. It was our routine to obtain a blood pressure and pulse on patients, and hers were on the boil. She was a sales clerk in an upscale department store and had come to the clinic to have sutures removed from a small laceration. Her wound was well healed, but her blood pressure was dangerously high, and her pulse was running like a racehorse. What could be wrong, I wondered.

Beth denied a history of heart disease or other disorders. She even bragged that she was so fit that she could work over a hundred hours a week at two jobs! I told her I could hardly keep up with my one job and asked, "How do you manage two?"

She paused, took a big breath, and then asked if taking drugs could affect her heart, her blood pressure, and her pulse. When I responded in the affirmative, she admitted to consuming increasing amounts of methamphetamine (a stimulant) to stay awake at her work. Her breakfast most mornings was coffee—no cream and two lumps of drug.

Why was she killing herself by working two full-time jobs? Beth answered that her dream was to own her own boutique, and that she needed the extra income to get started. Unfortunately, her life's ambition almost became her death sentence. If she had persisted in her methamphetamine addiction her reward would not have been a boutique, but her own Little Bighorn. If a malevolent taskmaster had whipped her into working hundred-hour weeks, he would have been denounced as unjust and inhumane. Yet the cruel taskmaster was Beth herself. She had tried to quit doing drugs at the urging of family, friends, and workmates. But conventional treatments had failed.

"The doctors just substitute their drugs for the drug I'm hooked on," she lamented.

Some might call her drug addiction a form of workaholism. Others might brand it modern living or "modernitis." After Beth became my patient I began to recognize variations of her condition in others. The clinic seemed a perpetual parade of harried people, overextended single parents, moonlighting moms and dads, and disconnected families in which communication was consigned to hurried refrigerator notes. Many were so consumed with making a living that they had forgotten what it meant to live and communicate, much less to recognize spirituality. For some, our Western medicine worked; for others, the ten-minute appointment was a caricature of what healing should offer. For most, we could only hope that our attempts to treat symptoms were sufficient, even though we knew we were ignoring the underlying cause of disease. What about Beth, my patient on drugs? Where should I go to help her, dare I even try, when so many had failed before me? What did Native healing have to offer? First, some background.

Mind-menders

Native healers believe that the mind runs through the body with a profound effect on health. This mind-body connection has a spiritual element, loosely translated as a "sacred way of life" (wak'a in Quechua, while other tribes have synonyms; the Navajo use hozho). As the North Star guides travelers, wak'a guides Native healers in their healing. Separation from one's wak'a—separation from one's sacredness, as in the case of a young woman hooked on methamphetamine—inevitably leads to illness. A second important aspect of Native healing has to do with integrating the healing process into the entire community.

We acknowledge the strength of the Yoeme communities and endeavor to honor and share our Elders' wisdom for the future of our children. Through the services of our health programs, the Yoeme Nation shall live in balance and harmony with the sacred circle of life.

—Pascua Yaqui (Yoeme) Tribal Health Department, Tucson, Arizona

It is hard to imagine an Anglo-run county health department that would craft a mission statement centered upon the influence of the sacred and the community in health care—wak'a, as described by the Yoeme Nation healers in the modern

Southwest. Native healers are surprised when spirituality and health, holistic healing, and alternative medicine are mentioned in the modern media as the latest health innovations. All have been recognized as important by Native Peoples for generations. In fact, at one meeting with the Hopi people in northern Arizona, a colleague of mine was told, "If you are here to talk about Hopi health without our spirituality, there's the door you can leave through."

The powerful effect of spirituality

Of concern to Native healers is the way in which practitioners of Western medicine, even the leaders of integrative and alternative medicine, generally limit their health advice to individuals. Native healers explore and promote the powerful effects of spirituality, family, and community on personal health. When I worked in the reservations of Northern Arizona I was struck by the influence of family and clan ties during routine medical visits. It was even considered rude to ask patients about a symptom without first learning about who they were. This entailed asking them to tell much more than just their names, and the conversation usually followed a pattern like this:

"What is your clan?"

"What clan are you 'born to'?" (This referred to the other side of the family.)

"What do you do for a living?"

"Who lives with you?"

"What do you live for?"

Only at this point could one proceed to the usual medical questions. (In emergency or life-threatening situations, more brevity was allowed.)

How are Native healing practices used to restore healing and well-being in this context?

How is wak'a or spirituality restored? What would it require to get Beth, my methamphetamine-addicted patient, back on course?

Native healers recognize there are two kinds of recovery required for healthful living. In Beth's case the first, and most obvious, was physical recovery from the biological effects of disease, addiction, and fatigue. The second was mental serenity, the release from a self-inflicted compulsion, the rest that follows the completion of a task, a psychological reward for a job well done, and an inner sigh of relief from affliction.

Inside your own head

Native healers believe that when things don't get better, the solution may be inside your own head, within your soul. For centuries they have practiced healing based on this belief. And, as we have seen, recent research shows that a spirit of optimism can be just as powerful as diet and exercise in preventing heart disease. Native healers believe you have everything you need, and that a healing spirit runs through the body, and now science lends credence to folklore. Native practices to promote psychological recovery may include the following strategies:

- Finding and remedying the true cause of illness.
- Developing a personal vision of well-being.

My patient Beth found relief from her condition by doing some simple, practical exercises.

Practical exercise for healing habits

What if you cannot find a Native healer, or if you could (see endnotes for resources, websites, and other reading), the idea makes you a little uncomfortable? You might be concerned about what your friends or business associates might think. Try the following exercise on your own.

PRACTICAL SUGGESTION

Reflection technique: creating a vision of well-being on your own

A sense of well-being means more than plopping our feet on the ottoman once a week. It means placing our minds and hearts into a higher state of being, an inspired rest that helps us free ourselves from spoiling our lives with emptiness or substance abuse or self-indulgence. It is a release from the captivity of our self-defeating ways. We will know such a feeling when we have an inner peace and satisfaction at the day's end.

In the fullest meaning of the word, well-being, like everything worthwhile, requires frequent practice. "What if I don't have a whole day?" many people ask. My answer: Almost everyone can find ten minutes to walk up and down the block, whistle a tune, say a prayer, sing a song, call a friend, or reflect.

EXERCISE: Reflection

Knowing how to reflect is an easy-to-learn technique. I tried this with Beth to settle her thoughts and strengthen her resolve to beat her case of modernitis.

The trick is to sit as comfortably as possible and close your eyes, concentrating only on breathing. With each breath taken, repeat in your mind the words "I AM," and on each exhalation the word "RELAXED."

This exercise should be repeated for at least five minutes. It can be done while waiting at the doctor's office, or when composing one's thoughts for an important business call, or during pre-takeoff jitters on board an airliner, but *not* while driving.

As UN-busy as a Bee

Some individuals cannot relax without psychological or psychiatric intervention. They suffer from the mania phase of a condition known as manic-depression, a mental disorder characterized by an elevated mood and mental and physical hyperactivity. Fortunately, this condition is unusual. For most of us the secret to effective relaxation is no secret—just to keep on practicing. It's like playing the piano; after a while, a pleasant tune emerges. Remember that even the honey bee, that model of energy and activity, has been shown in recent animal time studies to spend plenty of time just loafing—being as unbusy as a bee.

North: finding the true cause of an illness

Dreams may come

In Western culture, sleep is considered a refuel for the next day's activities—wasted time that could be used for other, more productive activities. In Native cultures sleep and dreams are an important component of health and self-awareness. Sigmund Freud wins the honors for bringing the interpretation of dreams to the forefront of Western psychology. For millennia Native healers have encouraged the use of dreams as a valuable healing tool. An extended search for inner meaning, involving the use of dreams, is called a vision quest. Modern science validates much of Native Peoples' understanding of the value of dreams and visions. In fact, medical research has shown that the lack of dreams is associated with certain pathological conditions.

> *"Whatever you need to know, dreams can reveal."*
> —Andean healer

Dreams often act out a resolution of internal conflicts. One patient with recurrent nightmares who underwent guided dream analysis found her night terrors revealed abuse as child. This intensely personal history had been long suppressed, and it seriously hampered her ability to establish a long-term, healing relationship with another person who eventually became a loving spouse.

PRACTICAL SUGGESTION

Keep a pen and paper by your bedside. Write down your dreams when you arise from sleep; it's far easier to remember them then than later. Once you are truly awake, read what you've written. Does anything make sense or guide your path? You might be surprised at the answers.

During a vision quest Native Peoples carry out an extended version of this process. The forty days of solitude spent by Moses on the mountain and by Jesus in the wilderness are Semitic versions of the same experience.

What are some practical suggestions and personal habits to help maximize healing in your own life?

Remember my "modernitis" patient? Self-induced stress and misplaced spirit were killing her until she learned to redirect her life. I have another patient who found a renewed spirit after the 9/11 terrorist attacks, and his stress headaches disappeared: "I don't have stress anymore—there are people with real problems out there," he said.

> *"You Westerners miss half of life—your dreams. Use them to your will."*
> —Andean healer

Maple as a cure

Maple syrup was originally produced by the Indians of the St. Lawrence River and Great Lakes region. It is created from the sweet watery sap of the sugar (Acer saccharum) *and the black* (Acer niger) *maple that is concentrated through evaporation. Native Peoples would lightly sweeten water with maple syrup to soothe an irritable baby (don't substitute honey in children under one year of age because of bacterial concerns). Maple leaves on the forehead, chest, or wrists offer cooling relief, too.*

Stress *or* distress

Stress is the body's natural response to "danger." Early humans developed a "fight or flight" response to hazardous situations. Ever hit the brake pedal to avoid a wreck and feel tingling in your face and arms and legs? That's the sudden surge of adrenaline, a stress hormone that allows your body to react, and to survive. What about the stressors of modern living? Maybe you are worried about your job, a relationship, children or grandchildren, or the lump under your skin? Sometimes a very simple thing, such as a touch of sweetness on the tongue, has a calming effect.

Stress *versus* distress

Life is chock full of events and changes that cause stress. Unlike early man, we usually can't just run away. Instead we internalize stress, and therein lies the problem. Much of what I see in my clinic is a parade of stressed patients. If they are injured, they get paid workers' compensation, often only a fraction of the income they ordinarily make. Unfortunately, their mortgages or rent and other bills don't take a holiday. So stress mounts, and they lose sleep, which slows their recovery and their return to work at full pay, and finally to a state of less financial stress. It's a vicious circle of stress.

Stress isn't all bad; it can help you rise to the occasion, or get a project completed. The key to healing is to separate stress from distress. When stress resolves, we relax. When we are under distress we don't. The body reacts negatively with muscle tension, headaches, and elevated blood pressure and pulse. I do maximal treadmill stress tests to determine heart function during strenuous exercise. The patient's pulse, blood pressure, exertion level, and electrical heart rhythms are continually monitored. Interestingly, the patient's pulse and heart rate go up while he or she is standing still, listening to me review the test, and they go down when the person starts exercising! Worry about the test while resting is more stressful than the vigorous activity of walking on a treadmill.

What do Native healers have to offer?

We can deal with stress, even use it to our advantage. Once a Native healer and I were sitting waiting for a conference to begin on the subject of government reimbursement of Native healers. He seemed relaxed and calm. I was impatient, cursing the tardy moderator. The healer's eyes seemed to flutter.

"Are you asleep?" I asked.

"No, I'm using the other side to relax," he answered calmly.

"What if you fall asleep?"

"Someone like you always wakes me up!" We laughed together. Here are his methods, which also helped my patient Beth to "glue" herself back together again.

PRACTICAL SUGGESTION

Stress busters

1. Take small breaks. Relax where you are. Close your eyes, and breathe deeply and slowly. Picture a relaxing setting, a sunset, a waterfall, or your own personal sanctuary.

2. Break it up. Go for a walk, somewhere to yell or cry. Some people talk to a friend or relative. Native Peoples may converse with a departed relative and conclude, "Grandmother would ignore that," or some other perspective-enlarging thought.

3. Ask yourself: "Ten years from now, will this matter?" Usually the answer is no. Native Peoples say: "To regain perspective, think of seven generations from now."

4. Focus on the positive. Say, "Good will come." Negative thoughts can affect vital organs, such as your heart, and lead to tension headaches and other conditions.

5. Remember, it's not what happens to us, but our interpretation of what's going on that truly matters.

6. Don't expect perfection. Anticipate that you will have problems and learn from them. Navajo weavers often leave a flaw or break in the design on a rug to remind us that only God creates perfection.

7. Accept what cannot be changed. If it is beyond your control, accept it. "Give unto Caesar that which is Caesar's," says the Bible (Luke 20:25).

8. Join something. Create a support system before you need it. Make time to be with people with whom you feel comfortable. Let friends help you when you are stressed. Return the favor when they're overloaded. Males often forgo such friendships and suffer because of it. Call an old friend. Don't just say, "Let's get together sometime." Be specific, and offer a date and a restaurant. Buy him or her lunch, or bring it to his or her office (and suggest turning off all phones).

PRACTICAL SUGGESTION

If the North pathway is true, and the spirit runs through the body—what Native Peoples call wak'a—then diaphragmatic breathing should work to release negativity.

Diaphragmatic breathing

Exhale completely—*push out bad thoughts.*

Inhale deeply and slowly through your nose, expanding your ribcage and then your chest. Count 1-2-3-4, and pause to *breathe in good thoughts.*

Exhale completely and slowly through your mouth, count 1-2-3-4, and pause.

Silently repeat a phrase or sound. I usually advise the word *"relax."* One patient liked "wak'a" because it sounded like a breath in ("wak") and out ("ah").

Allow other thoughts to enter and exit your mind, without focusing on them. Whenever other thoughts intrude, return your focus to the repetition of the word you've chosen, such as "relax."

Later, if you are in a stressful situation, simply repeat the chosen word for a calming effect.

The other pathways can be used in conjunction (you will find more details in the next chapters) as follows:

West: restoring healing balance

Progressive relaxation

Tighten the muscles in your feet for fifteen to twenty seconds, and then completely relax them.

Repeat with the muscles in your calves, thighs, and stomach, and end with the muscles in your face and head.

Try to consciously feel the difference between the tensed state and the relaxed state.

South: space and place in health or hozho

Hozho is a Navajo word for enjoying the beauty of an environment and seeking inner harmony. "Walk in beauty" is a Navajo saying that urges all people to appreciate their surroundings.

Guided imagery

Begin with diaphragmatic breathing to clear your mind and body of all your cares and tensions.

Reach for hozho: Picture a scene that you find very relaxing and soothing. It could be a quiet sandy beach on a summer day, an autumn forest with a deep bed of red and yellow leaves, a mountaintop overlooking a snowy valley, or a gentle summer rainstorm.

Imagine yourself entering one of these scenes and experiencing all of the sights, smells, sounds, and feelings.

East: the power of relationships

Support groups, counseling, or confidential sessions with a trained therapist can help:

Resolve personal problems or life crises.

Cope with and adjust to life pressures.

Deal with problems stemming from medical or physical concerns.

Teach skills to optimize personal effectiveness.

And sometimes the answer is medication, such as anti-anxiety or depression medicine. For this, seek help from a professional.

And what happened to Beth? Along with using these and other techniques to improve the health of her mind and body, she successfully completed a program called Recovery Together that promoted the power of healing relationships in the context of her family. We'll look at Recovery Together in more detail in Chapter 9.

Resources

www.ars-grin.gov/duke (Agriculture Research Service, for plant information)

www.consumerlabs.com (Database for label accuracy)

http://dietary-supplements.info.nih.gov (Dietary supplement information)

www.nccam.nih.gov (National Center for Complementary and Alternative Medicine)

Blumenthal M et al., editors. Herbal medicine: the expanded Commission E monographs. Newton (MA): Integrative Medicine Communication;2000.

Brown, DJ. Herbal prescriptions for better health. Roseville (CA): Prima Publishing;1997.

Burkhardt MA, Nagai-Jacobson MG. Dealing with spiritual concerns of clients in the community. J Community Health Nurs. 1985;2:191-198.

Carter TM. The effects of spiritual practices on recovery from substance abuse. J Psychiatr Ment Health Nurs. 1998;57:5-15.

Chandler E. Spirituality. Hospice J 1999;14:63-74.

De Marco DB. Medicine and spirituality. Ann Intern Med. 2000;133:920-921.

Duke, JA. The green pharmacy herbal handbook. New York: St. Martin's;2002.

Fehring RH, Miller JF, Snow C. Spiritual well-being, hope, depression, and other mood states. Oncol Nurs Forum. 1997;24:663-671.

Foster S. A Medicinal plants and herbs. New York: Houghton Mifflin;2002.

_______. The herbal drugstore. New York: Barnes & Noble Digital;2002

_______. Herbs for your health. Loveland (CO): Interweave Press;1996.

Glisson J et al: Review critique, and guidelines for the use of herbs and homeopathy. Nurse Pract 24:44,1999.

Graedon, J, Graedon, T. Dangerous drug interactions. New York: St. Martin's;1999.

__________________. The people's pharmacy. Rev. ed. New York: St. Martin's;1997.

Herford T, ed. Pirke avot: sayings of the fathers. New York: Schocken Books;1991.

Johnson, L. Pocket guide to herbal remedies. Malden (MA): Blackwell Science;2002.

Joyce CRB, Welldon RMC. The objective efficacy of prayer: a double blind clinical trial. J Chron Dis. 1965;18:367-377.

King DE, Bushwick B. Beliefs and attitudes of hospital inpatients about faith healing and prayers. J Fam Pract. 1994;39:349-352.

Kubzansky LD, Sparrow D, Vokonas P, Kawachi L. Is the glass half empty or half full? A prospective study of optimism and coronary heart disease in the normative aging study. Psychosom Med. 2001;63:910-6.

McGuffin M et al., editors. American Herbal Products Association botanical safety handbook. Boca Raton (FL): CRC Press;1997.

Multidimensional measurement of religiousness/spirituality for use in health research: a report of the Fetzer Institute/National Institute on Aging Working Group. Kalamazoo, MI: John A Fetzer Institute;1999.

Murray JE. Surgery of the soul: reflections on a curious career. Canton (MA): Science History Publications;2001.

Pizzorno J, Murray M. Encyclopedia of natural medicine. Roseville (CA): Prima Publishing;1998.

Post SG, Puchalski CM, Larson DB. Physicians and patient spirituality: professional boundaries, competency, and ethics. An Intern Med. 2000;132:587-583.

Pulchalski CM, Romer AL. Taking a spiritual history allows physicians to understand patients more fully. J Palliat med. 2001;3:129-137.

Reed PG. Religiousness among terminally ill adults. Res Nurs Health. 1987;9:35-41.

Sloan RP, Bagiella E, Powell T. Religion, Spirituality and medicine. Lancet 1999;353:664-667.

Sulmasy DP. Is medicine a spiritual practice? Acad Med. 1999;74:1002-1005.

Zink T, Chaffin J: Herbal 'health' products: what family physicians need to know. Am Fam Physician 58:1133, 1998.

8

Inside a Sweat Lodge: a history

If finding is the end of searching, it is better to go on searching.

— Rabbi Richard Safran

Early morning summer sunlight streamed in a brilliant yellow haze through the torn, dusty curtains of Room 4 at the Dinetah Motel and it was already unbearably hot. The sheer curtain fabric hung haphazardly at the window, with half the curtain-hooks missing. A speckled lizard slithered sideways up the wall by the window.

Rachel wanted to scream, but what good would it do?

She recoiled from the light and the lizard. She had a feeling that this was not going to be a good day, even though she had worked so hard to find this place with its healing possibilities. But she got out of bed and picked up her cotton slacks and blouse, shaking them to make sure there weren't any spiders or lizards. As Rachel dressed, she stood in front of a mirror that divided her young-for-late-thirties face with a two-inch crack. She looked and felt like a wilted plant, and she wondered if her impetuosity had gotten the best of her this time.

She was here in a remote corner of northern Arizona for a sweat lodge conducted by a Navajo healer, which she had heard might be a wonderful opportunity for people like her who had tried every possible treatment to recover from chronic pain. Lord knew she had endured them all without success: narcotics, anti-inflammatory drugs, antidepressants, injections, physical therapy, manipulation, body work, and rest.

Although she felt quite alone in such a remote, desolate place, Rachel was determined to investigate this health-restoring possibility. A reliable source had recommended the healer. Perhaps Rachel's family and friends would even congratulate her on being so brave?

Rachel counted the money she had left on the rough, splintering dresser. After paying for roundtrip airfare, the taxi, meals in the airport, and lodging, she had sixty dollars. She carefully folded the bills. They were so greasy she wanted to wash her hands after touching them.

She looked at her clothes—limp and dirty from the dense humidity, a rarity in the desert except after yesterday's August monsoon rain. The motel advertised a laundry, but she couldn't afford it. At least she could rinse out her underwear in the sink. She twisted the one faucet, and out dribbled rusty water. She tried to turn it off, but couldn't. Totally discouraged, Rachel slumped down in a chair and covered her face with her hands. Tears streamed down her face.

What would happen to her? She wished she had asked her husband for help; he had money. No, she thought stubbornly. She was always asking some man to solve her problems. First it was her daddy, then her boyfriends, and then her husband. No, this time she was going to manage on her own! Somehow ... some way ...

Knock! Knock! The noise interrupted her thoughts.

The rickety doorknob jangled back and forth. So much for a lock, Rachel thought. Barefoot, she opened the door.

The darkest, largest American Indian man she had ever seen barged past her.

"What ... are you ... ? Who are you?" She gulped, not knowing whether to run or yell for help.

"I am Tony Yazzie!" he bellowed in a voice too loud for the smallish room. He set down a basket of oranges on her dresser, and then removed a wadded, gray tablecloth from one pocket in his trousers, and a fork and knife from the other. "Compliments of the *hataalii*, the healer," he said, smiling at her through two yellow teeth on the bottom row of his mouth. "She wishes to have words with you after breakfast about the sweat lodge,"

"What should I bring to the sweat lodge? Fruit, a salad?" asked Rachel.

"It is not a potluck. It is more important what you take from the sweat lodge," Tony said, turning and filling the doorway with a huge blackness. Before Rachel could respond, he had shut the wobbly door behind him, and his heavy footsteps boomed down the hallway.

Rachel devoured the oranges, which helped satiate her thirst and appetite. She then gave herself a sponge bath with the rusty water in the sink. The lizard crawled lazily around the faucet. She ignored it, and brushed her auburn hair, which was frizzy and tangled from tossing and turning all night.

She pulled it back off her face and tied it with a ribbon. In the mirror her eyes were large and green, but she looked thin, and her skin was unusually pale. She'd skip the makeup; it would just slide off in this heat, anyway. She still felt grimy, but it was the best she could do.

She slipped on her tennis shoes, and then, somewhat hesitantly, went to the motel office.

The manager's name was Mr. Zah, a Navajo who was two shades lighter and four sizes smaller than Tony Yazzie. He apologized with sincerity for the conditions at the motel. He had only just acquired it from a former owner who had abandoned the property.

"Here, I will give you something to drink," he said. "It will help your thirst." From a pitcher sitting on his desk he poured her a glass of dark liquid that he called "sun tea."

He offered to refund her room charge, but she declined.

"Thanks for the offer," she said, "but I'm sure you'll need the money to fix the place up."

They shared a laugh. And then Tony appeared. He was her ride to the sweat lodge. His vehicle had once been a blue pickup, but dried mud now covered it with a white-gray film. Tony turned the ignition. The engine hesitated, then started, and backfired. He shifted from first gear to second, and then to third, creating a hard, loud grinding noise each time, and veered into a road that quickly turned from rough asphalt into two dirt ruts. As the motel disappeared behind them, Rachel thought that surely the sweat lodge wasn't far away. They bounced along in the truck over hard, sandy ridges, plowing through shrubbery and stunted trees. The track was so overgrown one could hardly call it a road. The scorching heat felt as though it was singeing her skin.

Maybe if she concentrated on the scenery around her, she could forget about her dry, parched throat. This desert wasn't all that desolate, after all. It was quite colorful if you ignored the paucity of green. The sun was floating airily in a blaze of apricot, high above the horizon, and clouds billowed overhead, edged with pink and purple tints. Why, it was beautiful!

Suddenly the front wheels went out of control and the steering wheel jerked. They were driving in soft sand and the brakes felt like jelly. Rachel thought they were going to crash in the desert—alone and without water!

But eventually, in spite of her fears, Rachel safely reached the healer she had come to see, whose name was Annie. She was a Diné (Navajo) traditional healer, sometimes called a singer, and she specialized in sweat lodges for women like Rachel. Annie was particularly known for conducting the complex ritual of the *Hózhóójí* or Blessing Way Ceremony. Its other name is the Long-life Empowerment Ceremony because of its power to restore harmony, balance, fulfillment, and well-being, especially during life transitions. With its rhythmic ebb and flow of prayers and chants, this ceremony reaches into the soul. It is most moving for the person who chooses to be the "one-sung-over"—the recipient of the ceremony.

Annie summarized her work simply: "One hopes to live to an old age and to live a life guided by beauty, the Beauty Way." Rachel soon saw that beauty for Annie was very much more than skin deep. To walk in beauty, Annie explained, is to live a life of inner tranquility and fulfillment. The Beauty Way enables you to tap into the good that is all around you, to peel back your layers of lost hopes, fears and drudgery and live your dreams again. The healer or *hataalii* teaches you to call on the power of the good forces all around us, not just in the sweat lodge, but anywhere, anytime. Many participants hum or sing phrases of the Beauty Way on a daily basis as they work. It seems to hold them in balance and enables them to recruit the forces of benevolence and goodness in times of trouble.

Annie, though elderly, had a face uncreased by worry, a winsome smile that revealed her ability to see the humor in ordinary life, and the serenity of a grand lady who knew what she was all about.

"Just looking at her outward appearance," thought Rachel, "you might think that she is a woman of modest means, but when she speaks, her words are priceless."

"I love it that I want to do a prayer for you. We are made up of prayers," Annie explained. "With prayer we listen to what is really important inside of us and all around us—the Beauty Way."

And then she said a prayer for Rachel and the others who had gathered before the sweat lodge, including Mr. Q, another *Belagana* (White American) who was visiting from Tucson.

"I have experienced other prayers in other settings with suspicion," Mr. Q said later. "I was often convinced the prayer was not for my well-being, but for my conversion to the other's chauvinistic version of the Almighty. Not so with Annie. Her prayer asked that all of us would find our true selves and have the strength to hold on to that truth with both hands and never let it go."

Now Annie told her listeners that as a child she had been seriously injured.

"Then a healer injected her spiritual power into me, and I was healed," said Annie. That medicine woman became her role model.

Healers, she told them, had three additional abilities that went far beyond effecting a physical cure.

The first was empowerment. "Medicine people know prayers for empowerment," said Annie. "They can reach into the innermost person and enhance their innate abilities, hopes, and dreams."

The second ability was prevention: "Our sleep-dreams can foretell the future. Therefore future harms can be prevented."

At one time or another, most of us have had a dream that gave a preview into another's behavior, or foretold a circumstance. Annie believed that there is a special power in all of us to enhance our ability to prevent bad events if we only listen to our inner person, both conscious and unconscious.

The third ability, she said, was humor. Laughter is a proven stress reliever, and Native healers employ it generously. Before entering the sweat lodge, Annie told a joke about the hazards of miscommunication.

It seems a powerful chief became too elderly to ride his horse and decided to auction it. A U.S. Forest Ranger offered him $25 and no more.

The chief responded negatively: "He don't look good."

The ranger said: "You drive a hard bargain. I'll give you $50."

The chief shook his head and replied: "He don't look good."

"All right," said the frustrated ranger. "Seventy-five dollars and that's my final offer!" He led the horse away.

Two weeks later the angry ranger confronted the chief: "What do you mean by selling me a horse that's blind!"

"I told you he don't look good," said the chief.

Laughing, Rachel lost some of her fear and doubt, as she had when she laughed in the motel office with Mr. Zah. Next Annie went on to say that she was also an herbalist and specialist in Native healing practices. She conducted programs that included counseling for domestic violence and substance abuse, based on indigenous teachings. Annie incorporated traditional methods with strategies for coping with modern living, and she recommended nine techniques to restore one to the Beauty Way.

"First, dedicate your sleep to gain knowledge," she said. Dreams can reveal a great deal about what troubles you.

"Second, close your eyes and you see better and hear better," she went on.

Third: "Ceremonies can remove obstructions." And ceremonies do not have to be elaborate, just something as simple as taking time each morning to feel the dawn.

This leads to the fourth technique. "Rise before sunrise and bathe in the coolness," said Annie. "It will help wash badness away, and you'll be able to handle any situation."

Fifth: "Smile about the problems you receive; they build muscle." Each of the challenges in her life had made her stronger and more capable, she thought. "Serendipity is around every corner and life detour," she said.

Sixth: "What's important is not what happened, but to rebuild."

Seventh: "Life is great, life is good, especially when you share it with someone."

Eighth: "I teach all the time," said Annie, "and I learn all the time."

Finally, the ninth technique was prayer. "When you pray long enough you will find shortcuts to the best path to take."

Now the time had come to enter the sweat lodge. "We Indians were forced to deny our culture and heritage, but we have a good message to share," Annie observed. "It keeps us strong, alert, and wise."

Rachel thought the sweat lodge looked like a canvas turtle. It was a rounded structure composed of branches covered with canvas or hides, with an opening to the east, as is traditional. In spite of the hot day, a fire burned outside the lodge, where large stones were heated, then brought inside to have water splashed on them to make the steam.

The air inside was as thick as a quilt, she thought.

The words Annie was speaking were unfamiliar, yet the rhythm seemed intensely personal. Rachel, Tony, Mr. Q, and the healer sat shoeless in a circle on cushioning robes on the ground. Their faces, illuminated by the red soothing glow of the hot stones, looked towards the center of the lodge. This circle gave Rachel a feeling of connectedness, even though the lodge experience was unfamiliar.

Offerings were made; prayers and chants were uttered and songs sung. At times herbs were placed on the fire outside or on the stones inside. Rachel smelled the distinctive juniper, an invigorating and comfortable odor that reminded her of her caring grandmother's nostrums when she was sick as a child.

When she was asked to share a good and pleasant memory, Rachel spoke of her grandmother.

"Do Navajo children participate in the sweat lodge?" she asked.

"The sweat lodge has too much power for young people," cautioned Tony.

"How old do you have to be?" asked Rachel.

"We use an ancient and very traditional Indian measure of maturity," said Tony, winking. She noticed that his left big toe peeked through a hole in his sock. "You must be old enough to drive a pickup truck."

Everyone laughed—again, the humor was a relief of the uncertainty that fills someone new to a sweat lodge, like Rachel and Mr. Q, and it gave them the message that it is best to be yourself and not overly serious even when you're ill.

"How is the sweat lodge different than the Scandinavian sauna?" asked Rachel, now more relaxed.

"Both of them purify and cleanse," said Annie as she poured more water on the hot stones. "But for us the sweat lodge is much more than that. It is a spiritual experience that brings us into harmony and balance with the world."

"What does that really mean?" asked Rachel.

"To bring a positive out of a negative. Fire is quenched by rain. The pain of childbirth is softened by the birth of a new life."

The healer paused, and then she looked deep into Rachel's eyes with an intensity that she never forgot. "It was as if she saw into my core," said Rachel later.

"I want to say a prayer for you," said Annie. "Later if you wish you can say your own prayer."

"I don't know if I have a prayer to say ... I haven't said one since I was a young girl in Sunday school."

"That is okay. With prayer we don't have to say anything. First we listen. We are made up of prayers. Yours will come."

She spoke in a chant:

"Yah hah ee yah yah.
"Yah hah ee yah yah
"Whey yeh yeh."

"We pray for Rachel who seeks healing," Annie continued, speaking English but still chanting. "Her pain is real; it has taken on a life of its own, but it is not her life." Then she went on, "Her life is one of harmony, of peace, of healing. Her pain will pass over her and through her with your help, Great Spirit. And she will laugh as it passes away."

And the healer repeated her first chant:

"Yah hah ee yah yah.
"Yah hah ee yah yah
"Whey yeh yeh."

"What pain brings you here, Rachel?" she said.

"My pain is chronic; it is always with me. Nothing helps for long. How did you know?"

"It is how you walk and sit. Many come here with such pain."

"Not like mine; there is nothing like it. Some days all I can do is eat and go back to bed."

"When did the pain begin?" Annie asked as Tony sprinkled more water on the stones. A swirl of steam circled around Rachel and whispered in her ears.

"Lifting my child out of her crib, I hurt my back ... I haven't been the same since."

"And your husband, where was he?"

"As usual, out of town. When I was pregnant with Chloe he promised to cut back on his out-of-town trips, but it never happened."

"And who has the baby now?"

"Since I've been hurt, he has had to stay home. I just can't lift her anymore."

"What would happen if your pain went away and you could lift Chloe again?"

"He would probably go back to his old ways."

"He has a name," said the healer, and her eyes narrowed into a critical slant.

"Of course. Jim."

"Have you ever told Jim about this, your feelings?"

"You know men. They don't like to talk."

"Yes, I know men, Rachel," Annie said, laughing with her like a conspirator. Tony chuckled as well. "I will say a prayer for you, Rachel. One that hopes you will live to an old age and a life guided by beauty—the Beauty Way, also known as hozho.

"Breathe in the dawn four times.
"Breathe out a prayer to yourself,
"To the dawn, the universe.
"It is holy, all holy once more."

"Now, Rachel, say your prayer ... what is in your heart."

"I don't usually pray ... "

"I can see a prayer in your face. Start with a few words. The rest will come out."

"God ... dear God help me. I've tried to be a good mother and wife, but sometimes I just can't do it all. It's so hard to do it alone." Tears streamed down her face. "This pain is ruining our marriage. We haven't been together physically as a couple for almost a year. I pray that Jim will understand that my pain is real, I did hurt myself, but I can't do it alone. If he'll just not travel so much and help out more ... "

"Go on, Rachel. God is listening."

"Jim, if you'll promise to help me, I think I can recover better." Rachel put her face in her hands and softly sobbed.

Time passed, but Rachel and Mr. Q did not notice how much time it was. Later, after more prayers, Rachel said she felt as if a tremendous weight had been lifted off her back, where she had felt so much pain before. She asked if Jim would think she was a fake, that she had planned an injury to get her way.

"I've never met a fake in a sweat lodge," Annie answered. "The roads are too bad here. They would give up before they got to me." Her kind wink gave Rachel permission to laugh and laugh, a deep soulful laugh that overcame the past and promised a better future.

"Rachel, the past is behind you. Do what you should do today. Tomorrow is a new dawn, a new beginning."

"I can't take the sweat lodge with me when I go home."

"You can. Rise early before the sun awakes, and face east. Let the cool morning air purify your thoughts. When the sun rises, feel its healing power just as you have felt it from the red-hot stones in our lodge."

Rachel stared longingly at the still-warm lodge stones whose heat combined with water had created the steam. "I'll remember that. Thank you."

Fingers of new light appeared in the sweat lodge. At first Rachel thought it was some outer expression of inner radiance around the attendees, but then the obvious explanation emerged. The night was over, and the sun was rising.

This is why lodges all have an opening to the east towards the rising sun. The Blessing Way includes the No Sleep, an all-nighter, and afterwards the subject of the sweat is given a medicine bundle that represents his or her new life.

Now the ceremony ended. The one-sung-over, Rachel in this case, rose as if following some voice that was both inside and outside the lodge, and she emerged reborn into the new light of the morning sun. She saw charcoal mountains topped with a starry crown. She breathed in four times and filled her body with a renewed spirit and harmony. Then a silver web of light spread over the peaks and absorbed her. "I'm free!" she gasped. "My back should be killing me, and I can hardly feel it."

Strangely, even after an all-night ceremony, Rachel and Mr. Q left with new energy rather than fatigue. Some participants in sweat lodge ceremonies report sleeping better afterwards, even months after, than they have in years.

And Rachel later reported to Tony Yazzie that the sweat lodge had helped her over the long term. For example, she and Jim had worked things out. Rachel still had to be careful to lift properly, and she continued to do her stretches and back exercises, but she was off the medicines except for an occasional tablet of ibuprofen.

A note on Rachel's history

Rachel's story of chronic illness is characteristic of many. Typically they involve:

- Multiple treatments. One patient summed it up as: "Been there, tried it, seen it, taken it."
- Discouragement.
- Disconnection from family members.
- Deeper issues that may not have caused the illness, but which magnify with time.
- Dependency. Sometimes it is easier to be ill. Recovery takes work and the recruitment of others.

Breaking a sweat in other traditions

Therapeutic, religious, and social bathing has a long tradition throughout the world. The most famous "bather" in the Judeo-Christian tradition is John the Baptist. John was practicing a version of *mikveh*, or Jewish spiritual immersion and renewal, when he encountered Joshua (Jesus' name before it was Hellenized) on the banks of the Jordan (John 1: 25-36). This was adapted into Christian baptism. In modern times, as we have seen, baptisteries have been added to many hospitals for spiritual purposes. For those whose tradition mandates total immersion, special devices have even been added to allow an immobile patient hooked up to life support to descend below the water. "At the moment of immersion," said one Jewish woman, speaking of the mikveh, "you are as close as you can ever be to God."

Many other parallels to sweat lodges may be found in non-Native American cultures. These include countless springs, sacred or otherwise, frequented by the Greeks and the Romans. Long ago, people noticed that the heat and minerals found in natural hot springs have an especially beneficial effect on some individuals. Many natural springs have become health spas famous for their hot or mineralized water (the term "spa" comes from the Belgian resort town of Spa, where mineral springs believed to have medicinal benefits were first discovered in 1326). Such treatments are still covered by Italian health insurance. In the United States the most famous historic frequenter of hot springs was probably Franklin Delano Roosevelt, who often sought relief for his polio-crippled legs at a spa in Warm Springs, Georgia, where eventually he died in 1945.

I live a mile from the Agua Caliente Spring ("hot water" in Spanish) in Southern Arizona. It is indeed relaxing to place feet tired from hiking into the hot water that bubbles up from the sand. Be careful, though, if you are wearing jewelry. While soaking with friends in the mineral springs of Rotarua, New Zealand, the new bride of one of my colleagues screamed. Her "fourteen-karat gold" wedding ring had just turned green. Its purity was doubtful.

Bathing also has a long tradition in Japan. While staying at a traditional Japanese hotel or *ryokan*, I was surprised to learn that the shower was for cleaning off the grime, and the bath to follow was for relaxation. I can still remember those long soaks, an ideal remedy for jet lag! Whirlpool baths, also relaxing, have a number of additional health-related benefits. I am the physician for 800 firefighters, who frequently suffer burns. Therapeutic whirlpools are one of the most effective methods to gently debride (or surgically remove) dead skin and to promote the growth of healthy new tissue.

Perhaps the most familiar steam baths are those that are found in health clubs, many hotels, and even homes. They are similar to sweat lodges in their use of steam and heat, though they lack the Native American spiritual component, as Annie pointed out. I did once encounter chanting in a sauna, but it was while trying to enjoy it with an inebriated rugby team. However, my Norwegian friend and fellow physician, Truls Ostbye, reminds me that the North American version of the sauna lacks the rigor of the original, which concludes with immersion in a freezing cold stream after the steam bath, to "close up the pores again." Less rigorous saunas appear to be beneficial to patients with heart arrhythmias (or irregular rhythms). At the annual meeting of the American College of Cardiology in 2002, Dr. Takashi Kihara reported that daily saunas decreased fatigue, shortness of breath, difficulty sleeping, and premature ventricular contractions (extra heartbeats).

Some Indian nations, particularly the Pueblo people, promote sacramental shampoos and include them in their ceremonies. "Renewal and rescue of split ends!" joked one tribal member. One such cleansing aid, which you can make on your own, is soapwort shampoo (see next page).

Of course the health benefits of bathing and of applying moist heat to the body are numerous. Conditions that may benefit from such treatment include:

Burns: Debridement of damaged skin and promotion of new skin. Note that in the very recent burn, when the skin is intact, cold is beneficial to counteract the retained heat in the burned cells, whose thermal energy can cause damage for a considerable time if not neutralized.

Muscle aches: Heat applied for twenty minutes, repeated several times a day, can relieve soreness.

Sprains (involve tendons) and strains (do not involve tendons): Usually ice is advised for ten minutes three to four times a day the first twenty-four hours. After that, many use "contrast" treatments that alternate ice with heat. If you use a heating pad, don't fall asleep on it, as you might sustain a burn from prolonged exposure.

Infections: Heat can "draw" an infection. For example, a foreign object lodged in the body can become infected. The theory is that heat can increase the

Soapwort shampoo

*Take the soapwort plant (*Saponaria officinalis, *also called bouncing bet), roots and all, and cover and soak in water for half an hour. (In the western United States, you can substitute yucca roots). Puree and strain through cheesecloth or a coffee filter. Warm it and work into your hair. Refrigerate the unused portion (lasts three to four weeks).*

blood flow of infection-fighting elements where they are needed. More reliably, heat kills microbes. This is why we have a fever when we have an infection. Sometimes patients are frantic when they have even a mild fever. In cases where it is mild (severe ones can cause febrile seizures), I reassure them that their body knows best, and that suppressing a fever might prolong their illness. Usually it is hard to compete against their television, which advises them to medicate everything with "the fever reliever doctors recommend most."

Sore throats: What about those old-fashioned saltwater gargles for sore throats? Heat and salinity both kill microbes. Call your doctor if a fever and swollen glands occur, or if pain worsens or persists.

Headaches: The warm washcloth or poultice on the head is a grandmotherly remedy. Does it help? Nobody knows, but I certainly have fond memories of my mother providing this remedy, and reading me a bedtime story. I might have improved without such ministrations, but as I've learned, caring is part of curing.

Most of us have headaches, but very few of them are serious. So why, I asked myself at one point, did I see so many people in the clinic with a minor condition that resolves rapidly? (This does not include those with vascular or migraine headaches or other more severe varieties.)

The third sacred pathway helped me understand. Most of the walking well with headaches were seeking reassurance that they didn't have a brain tumor. They needed a relationship with a healer who said the obvious: "You do not have a brain tumor, based on your history and my physical examination." Mostly when they heard the first seven words, they stopped listening. I do caution such patients that if the headache persists, or if other symptoms present themselves, then the person should call or page me immediately.

Psychological or spiritual renewal: Rachel's history illustrates one of the benefits of water, hot or steamed, in combination with other elements such as visualization of a better life path. Participants in a mikveh or a baptism will attest to their healing power of renewal.

PRACTICAL SUGGESTION

Create these benefits at home

How can you achieve these benefits at home? Here are some suggestions for creating your own "sweat lodge," even without sweating! What are the key elements of a sweat lodge? The experience of several simultaneous elements is more powerful than only one, but a singular component is better than none at all. Do the following:

1. Secure peace. Turn off the electronics (pager, telephones, cellphone). Don't answer the door.
2. Provide a rhythm. Healers use chants and songs. Radios or tape players will suffice. The sound of water falling works. Or just hum or whistle to yourself.
3. Put something on your skin. Try steam, a wet washcloth, a heating pad, a bath.
4. Focus. Think of the most relaxing place where you have ever been. Say a word over and over again. "Relax" is easy. Then breathe in, and think "I am . . . " Breathe out, and think " . . . relaxed."

For Native Peoples the sweat lodge is a place for warm steam bathing, spiritual renewal, prayers, and healing. Sweat lodges are usually constructed of saplings or flexible branches tied together and covered with skins, canvas, or old quilts, with an opening facing east. Heated rocks are brought inside, and water is sprinkled periodically on them to create steam. One aromatic addition is peppermint leaves, which also make a soothing tea. If mixed with strawberry leaves, the combination aids indigestion. (I grow both plants in my garden.)

Precautions

Avoid a sweat lodge if you are very young (you must have your driver's license, according to Tony Yazzie!) or pregnant, or if you have any conditions affecting your heart, lungs, neurological system, electrolyte balance, or metabolic system (thyroid, for example).

Always be certain the sweat lodge has good air circulation, and also be certain to maintain adequate hydration. A good rule of thumb is: "Keep your pee pale." Half-strength sports drinks such as Gatorade can help you keep your electrolytes in balance. An easy substitute that we used in Somalia, where sports drinks are not available, is to add a handful of sugar and a pinch of salt to a liter or quart of water, then stir and drink.

And finally, only participate in a sweat with someone you trust, or based on a recommendation from someone trustworthy.

Peppermint / Strawberry Tea

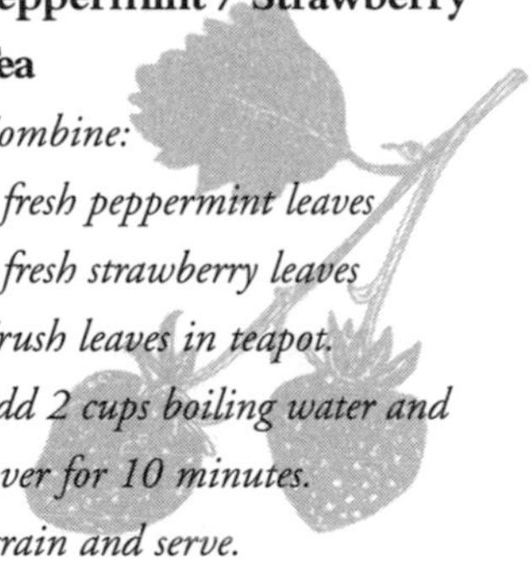

Combine:
8 fresh peppermint leaves
4 fresh strawberry leaves
Crush leaves in teapot.
Add 2 cups boiling water and cover for 10 minutes.
Strain and serve.

9

East: the second pathway

The power of relationships — healing as a group activity

Disease prevention may be accomplished by the application of three major strategies: self-help, the medical model employing the assistance of a professional practitioner, or communal action.
—R. A. Stallones, M.D.

After reading this section or pathway you will understand:

1. How Native healers and practices
   - Promote healing and connecting with community and family
   - Utilize the healing power of ceremony
   - Develop healing partnerships
2. And you will understand how to use practical suggestions and personal healing habits to maximize healing in your own life.

The January diet: develop healing partnerships

Ever start on a diet in January to shed some of your holiday-acquired fat? Usually, after a week or two of determination, your individual efforts fail. "No man is an island," said the English poet and preacher John Donne. Native healers recognize the power of relationships in healing. Modern psychologists who promote support groups for breast cancer and other illnesses and conditions have learned what Native healers have always known and practiced: The power of one grows greater when united with the whole. What does that mean? Consider exercise programs. The Centers for Disease Control and Prevention advise twenty to sixty minutes of daily physical activity. You decide to jog. Inevitably you're too tired, just don't feel like it, are bored, stop going as often, and quit.

	NORTH	EAST	WEST	SOUTH
	Sun Duality of light (wave & particle) and humans	Wind Sacredness of words	Rain Life-giving	Earth
ACTION	*Know* Spirit runs through the body	*Understand* Power of relationships	*Build* Healing partnerships	*Create* Harmony with life cycle space/place
DESCRIPTION	Holistic approach Humans are more than a list of physical complaints	Group therapy Group support *No man is an island.*	Doctor-patient relationship Patient-centered care	Self actualization Homeostasis
NATIVE WORDS	Wak'a Care for/treat the soul	Talking stick, Talking circle Words of all heard with respect	Katsinam Convey individual comments/prayers to gods	Hozho Place of beauty (inner harmony)
ICON	Sun	Sweat lodge	Katsina	Sand painting
PATIENT ENCOUNTER	Doctor listens at a deeper level	Understands context of patient's family and community	Patient is center of healing, not to *do* to, but to heal *with*	Convert illness to harmony
EXAMPLE	Male with low back pain, won't go to work. Tests normal.	Wife with cocaine habit. He must stay home.	He could have gone to work, lost wife. Instead she joins Cocaine Anonymous.	He joins co-dependent group. He returns to work.
THERAPEUTICS	Discover true cause of illness	Engage family and co-workers	Develop synergy with patient	Restore natural life cycle

Try exercising with your spouse, a friend, or a colleague. Two remarkable things will happen. First, the commitment to meet someone else for the designated activity will propel you to get out of bed, stop what you are doing, etc. When you're down, they're likely to be up. Together, both of you are more likely to continue. Second, the psychological benefits are enormous. After our youngest could be left safely with our fourteen-year-old, my wife and I began to jog together again. It was like rediscovering an old friend, someone to talk with (we jog slowly) without interruptions by children or phones.

Practical exercise

Remember, it's physical activity, not equipment or athletic skill, that's essential. Gardening, trimming the hedges, and walking all count. When at home, avoid sitting on the couch. Keep moving, do a chore, etc. Consider buying a treadmill or similar device. You can't say it's too rainy to walk if you have one. If such a device is too boring, listen to music or read while you are working out.

Lift light weights (five pounds or two kilograms are sufficient) with many repetitions for the following reasons:

Muscle burns more calories than fat. Strength training makes it easier to lose and maintain a healthy weight

Moving even a light weight helps avoid the one percent per year decline in muscle mass and fifteen percent decrease in strength that tends to occur per decade after age fifty, followed by thirty percent per decade after age seventy. These declines contribute to injuries in the elderly.

Exercise excuses

1. *"I don't have time to exercise."*
2. *"I don't like to exercise."*
3. *"I'm too tired at the end of the day."*
4. *"I'm too heavy and too old."*

Sound familiar?

Responses

1. Do you have time to brush your teeth? Add physical activity to your daily routine to add life to your years and years to your life.
2. Don't exercise, just avoid sitting all day. If you are at home, keep moving, walking, etc.
3. Try physical activity before you go to work. You'll find you have more energy all day.
4. Regular physical activity offers innumerable benefits to older and heavier adults. The Harvard Alumni Study even found an increase in longevity for those who didn't start regular exercise until their seventh decade!

The benefits of exercise include:

- Potential decrease in colon, rectal, breast, prostate cancer
- Less osteoporosis, or thinning of the bones
- Fewer hip and vertebral fractures
- Decrease in Diabetes Type 2
- Improved blood pressure
- Decreased symptoms of congestive heart failure
- Improved lipids (cholesterol)

PRACTICAL SUGGESTION

Four easy exercises you can do almost anywhere

First consult your doctor to be sure you don't have any contraindications to exercise, such as cardiac conditions, including a recent change in an electrocardiogram (EKG), heart attack, unstable angina, acute congestive heart failure, out-of-control high blood pressure or metabolic disease, third-degree heart block, valvular heart disease, cardiomyopathy, or complex ventricular ectopy.

Exercise 1
Chair squats: Sit, lean slightly forward, stand up.

Exercise 2
Shoulder shrugs: Stand, hold a book in each hand,
shrug shoulders, lower shoulders.

Exercise 3
Biceps curl: Hold book or other weight in each hand,
bend arms at elbow, lift weights to shoulders, lower them.

Exercise 4
Wall push-up: Stand 2-3 feet from wall,
place hands on wall, lean body to wall,
push body away from wall.

How to build a healing relationship—table talk

An American Indian tradition helps people of all ages connect, share, and receive useful advice. Many Native Peoples use an ancient practice known as the talking circle to listen to each other, explore inner and external threats to well-being, and cement personal bonds. How does it work?

The talking circle begins with the lighting of cedar, sweet grass, and sage to cleanse the body, renew the soul, and promote good energy. A stick—decorated with beads and seashells—is passed around the room. The rules are simple. Everyone takes a turn. When you hold the stick, everyone else listens, and no one else talks.

Drugs and sticks

Sky was a fifteen-year-old troubled teen who was using drugs. His parents, like many in our society, were consumed with the job of making ends meet, and they rarely talked with Sky except to remind him about undone chores. They never discussed relationships or illegal drugs.

Unfortunately, Sky was surrounded by a drug culture. Kids everywhere were using, abusing, and distributing chemicals. Older drug-dealing teens would often give away free samples of cocaine and other highly addictive drugs to younger, vulnerable potential customers in a deadly marketing ploy. Once the new user was hooked on the freebies, the dealer required payment, and the teen had to steal to support the habit.

We arranged for Sky to join a talking circle. This was a way to connect to another culture where no stigma was attached to seeking help. This method also is open to all, regardless of their religious or other beliefs. Sky didn't always speak when it was his turn to hold the talking stick, but soon he found it easier. Something resonated inside him. He said he "had all these words and feelings that wanted out," but he had no way or means to release them except through the ever-pervasive drugs of our Western culture.

With the help of the talking circle, he is no longer using drugs, and he invites his friends to participate. Many who attend the circle are teenagers who come from abusive homes; others are just neglected by a parent or parents.

PRACTICAL SUGGESTION

How can this help you connect with others or build a healing relationship?

If you are like most of us, your most precious commodity is time. You ask: "Who has time for a lengthy discussion with their children? If I had the time, where do I begin? I'm not a counselor." Others are intimidated by the modern media. How can you compete against attention-grabbing entertainment for your kids' minds?

Experts like David Lynn, M.Ed. (part Cherokee and a nationally recognized youth counselor training expert) will tell you:

- Keep it fun by using simple, easy-to-play games such as telephone.
- Make it meaningful. Kids really do worry and think about serious themes.

Table talk

Where can you start? Try this. I call it table talk. Let's say your children are having a difficult time cooperating together. Initially you choose to nag: "Why can't you kids get along?" But kids tune out for several reasons. First, you've offered no practical solutions or steps to reach the goal of getting along. Second, kids become parent deaf. They've heard it all before, so repetition is wasted, and if it hasn't worked before, why now? Third, your message is boring. Fourth, there is no logical consequence for not changing the behavior. What's a parent to do?

Rule One: keep it fun

Start with a warm-up game. A good icebreaker is to play telephone. Make it goofy. Whisper, "Granddad wears ice cream on his head!" in the ear of the person next to you. Have each person repeat what he thought he heard to the next one. The only guarantee in this book is that the last person to hear the message won't recognize the original one.

Now that they have warmed to working on a family exercise like telephone, advance to a cooperation game. Don't call it that, or you'll spoil it. Call it the Mummy Wrap instead. (This one works for ages six to fourteen.)

Mummy Wrap rules

Give your "Junior Archaeologists" a roll of toilet paper.

Tell them they have seven minutes to choose someone to wrap up like an Egyptian mummy. Although many Plains People wrapped their dead and placed them on raised platforms (a partial mummification), use the more familiar Egyptian model.

If they ask about the other rules, such as how to pick the child to wrap, tell them it's up to them to decide how to work together.

Time's up. Admire their creation. One group used a marker to paint fake eyelashes and hoop earrings on the face wrap of the mummy.

Ask how they decided whom to wrap, who would wrap what part, and so on. And how do they think they would do it differently next time?

Punch line question: What did you think you learned about cooperation? How do you think we can work together better to cooperate as a family?

Notice I included "you think" in the questions. If you read the two preceding questions without those two words, they sound like a teacher waiting for an answer, instead of a query from one member of a group who values the ideas of the others.

Rule Two: make it meaningful

Remember that Native Peoples say that stories give strength and meaning to our lives.

If you've still got their interest and want to build on a theme, consider three other options or additions. All of these techniques can help people open up and speak about what's on their minds.

Option one

Read a story of cooperation. I've successfully used this one about the Special Olympics.

The Special Olympics story

A group of young boys and girls with Down's Syndrome (characterized by mental retardation and physical changes) were lined up for a race at the Special Olympics. The race began, but halfway through one boy stumbled and fell flat on his face. The others slowed, stopped, and then returned to the fallen boy and helped him up. They all held hands and finished the race together. The crowd went wild with applause for the youngsters.

Table talk

Ask questions such as these: How do you think the boy felt when he fell? How about later? What do you think the adults and others learned from this story? How do you think the children felt who went back for the boy to help him up? Do you think any of them missed not getting first prize in the race because they stopped to help another?

And finally: Do you think what they learned is something we can use in our lives, in our family?

Option two

Describe a moral dilemma and ask kids what they would do.

Lost and found

On his way to school Ryan found a wallet containing several dollar bills. What should he do? What do you think you would do?

Option three

Play the talking card

Use this one if your family has a problem with interruptions while others are speaking. You can also make your own talking stick. In our family we use a wooden spatula sometimes when we can't find the family talking stick (known as the hiding stick because it disappears so often).

Take a large card, fold it in the middle, and write "Listen" on one side and "Talk" on the other.

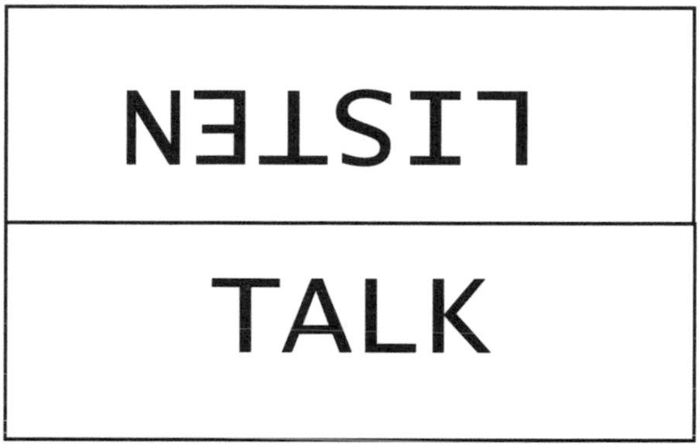

Two participate. Each only sees his/her side of the card. On the Talk side of the card write one or more of the items below.

"A thing I'm proud of is ... "

"One thing I'd do differently is ... "

First the person on the talk side offers his or her thoughts. Now switch the card, so the Listener becomes the Talker who speaks on the same topics

Parent values

Do kids really care about their parents' beliefs or standards? The studies show convincingly that they do. Your response now may be, "Not that I would ever know it!" But you will, if you attempt the easy-to-do, user-friendly exercises above.

"Jail! For drugs?" or how to build a positive counterculture

"My daughter Larisse is in jail for drugs!" exclaimed a patient named Claire. "I don't know how it could have happened. Not to my daughter."

"Did you have any clue about Larisse from her behavior?" I asked.

"Not really. I thought it was the usual high school stuff, talking back, new friends. I'd constantly have to remind her to do things, and then her grades dropped. The worst was the secretiveness."

"Secrets? What kind?"

"Where she's going, who with, how late. That sort of thing."

Claire was seeing me for a musculoskeletal injury, but it was obvious at our many follow-up sessions that her mind and the delayed recovery of her body were tied to her daughter's drug use. She became consumed with nagging, lecturing, bribing, and penalizing Larisse—to no avail. It was also painfully evident that Western drug rehabilitation approaches were failing with her daughter, who had now dropped out of school.

Recovery Together

At this point Dave Lynn, M.Ed., who is part Cherokee, and his colleague William Inboden, D.O., promoted another pathway—the power of relationships and healing as a group activity. Their approach, an integral part of their program called Recovery Together, fits into the concept of the East pathway. (Remember Beth, our methamphetamine-addicted salesperson? She participated successfully in this program.)

Recovery Together exists as a learning community of young people and their parents that promotes clean and sober living. The traditional approaches to treatment consist of various ways to reinforce controlling young people's alcohol or other drug use. Teens are pushed prematurely into committing to lifelong abstinence from alcohol and drugs when they are not yet willing or ready to accept change. This forced commitment leads to unintended negative consequences, such as high rates of relapse, adolescent rebellion, and hurting parents. Parents usually have few skills to handle a son or daughter who continues using alcohol or other drugs. And the usual treatment programs offer little to parents in this regard.

Working with parents and their teenage children, the Recovery Together approach shifts the emphasis from attempting to control young people's alcohol or other drug use to changing the conditions in the family. Such an approach is compatible with the East or Second Pathway, which recognizes the power of personal or family relationships and healing as a group activity. Parents and young people participate together in learning the skills needed to create healthy conditions that protect themselves and their values from the ravages of substance abuse.

Recovery Together creates a learning community of young people and parents who work together for the common purpose of substance-free living. Both teens and their parents attend every session of the program together and work through a recovery theme each week. By attending a Recovery Together group, a family becomes part of a learning community that transforms their lives.

Healing partnerships for life

There are other vital healing partnerships available to us. Native healers believe our health and our spirits are connected not only to those around us, but also to those who have gone before—back to the beginning of creation. These connections to those with and within us, past and present, can be drawn upon for strength in time of illness, for inspiration to show us a better way, to find wellness, or to seek recovery from illness or addiction.

Expanded view of life

Native healers walk around with an expanded view of life. For Whites the argument is often whether "life" begins at conception. For the Native healer "this life" began generations ago and continues many generations hence.

"Every action should be taken with thoughts of its effects on children seven generations from now."
—Cherokee saying

More than genes?

How we respond to illness, whether we become ill in the first place, and if we will recover are all related to our background and our support systems.

Connections to others and to our past exist in every one of our 4.5 billion cells, in our genetic makeup. If you have any doubts, consider this—each of our cells has its own energy producers called mitochondria, and the DNA in mitochondria is transmitted from generation to generation. The latest research has now unequivocally proven that every human being is related to a single ancestral female. To no one's surprise, geneticists call her Eve.

The genetic revolution will change our lives as profoundly as the information/computer revolution did. However, our traits and behaviors are so multifaceted that it will not be possible to alter or prevent a condition such as cardiovascular disease by changing a single gene. For example, preventing diabetes will involve many genetic pathways. Our behaviors and our response to disease will also diminish the effectiveness of genetic engineering. One half of all deaths are caused by behavior whose genetic determinants are complex, difficult to alter genetically, and environmentally triggered. If you are prone to diabetes and your neighborhood school cafeteria offers high-carbohydrate foods (in some areas, one third of all the calories kids ingest come from soft drinks), you're in trouble. Gene therapy will not change the disease-promoting behaviors of peers. Neighbors and vendors, as well as a host of genes, would need to be altered to resist these negative influences.

Genogram

A key to understanding the power of behavior and relationships on your life is to recognize the influence of your past on your present—of "those who have gone before." This topic reminds me of LaVern, a Navajo healer I know who memorized the names of his ancestors for thirty generations back.

"Why bother?" I asked.

"Most Belagana (Whites) know the heritage of their dog better than themselves," he answered, chuckling.

True. I have a neighbor who has an American Kennel Club pedigree showing many generations of his dog's ancestors. Pitifully, I only know the names of one-fourth of my great-grandparents, just two out of eight.

The world from which we come

So what's all this have to do with keeping you whole and healthy? Try a genogram, a new approach to recording your family tree, and see if it helps you understand how you respond to stress and illness. Most family trees emphasize the roots and branches, but this one will reveal the fruits and nuts!

Practical Exercise

Write down traits of your family members, not just hair or eye color, but if they were optimistic or pessimistic, problem-solvers or critical. These descriptions are part of family lore: "Uncle John was the creative one." Enter both maternal and paternal personality traits. Here's mine:

PATERNAL	MATERNAL
Father: Loyal, loud, inclusive, depression with Lou Gehrig's disease	Mother: Kind, forgiving, inclusive, optimistic
Father's father (grandfather): Loyal, loud, honest, shell shock when gassed by Germans	Mother's father (grandfather): Entrepreneurial
His father: Loyal, entrepreneurial, grief-stricken and became an alcoholic when wife died	His father: ?
His mother: Loyal	His mother: ?
Father's mother (grandmother): Loyal, loud, family first, critical, resented move from Europe	Mother's mother (grandmother) Kind, forgiving, religious
Her father: ?	Her father Alcoholic
Her mother: ?	Her mother: Independent—first woman in the history of her county to ask for divorce (husband an alcoholic)

Now complete your personal genogram. Remember that stepparents can play a considerable role. Abraham Lincoln attributed his interest in learning to the positive influence of his stepmother, Sarah Bush Johnston Lincoln.

PATERNAL	MATERNAL
Your father	Your mother
Your father's father (your grandfather)	Your mother's father (your grandfather)
His father	His father
His mother	His mother
Your father's mother (your grandmother)	Your mother's mother (your grandmother)
Her father	Her father
Her mother	Her mother

Often genetics focuses on inherited conditions such as hemophilia, but knowing personality traits from your genogram can help reveal the answers to these questions:

- How will you respond to stress or illness?
- What are your coping strategies when sick?
- How easily can you gather the support of others when ill?
- Will others support the "healthier you" when you adopt healing measures, or will they compromise your change for the better?
- How will you usually respond to their opinions when they aren't supportive?

Practical value of a genogram?

My wife's grandmother had a hardscrabble life. Her husband was crippled from rheumatoid arthritis at an early age, so she had to work at a menial job to support the two of them and their young son (my father-in-law). During the toughest times, when food was short, she would say, "Life's deepest sorrows are spent in self pity," and she would keep plugging along. My wife says that any time she has suffered a failure or feels like quitting she remembers Grandma Lucia's words and finds the strength to move ahead.

A genogram can heighten your ability to respond to illness or other life events by making you aware of "trait pitfalls," disease tendencies, the need for preventive support from your family or others, and an inner "inherited core of strength" as well. Here's an example.

Death by doughnuts

Mr. G, newly diagnosed with diabetes, asked, "How should I respond as a diabetic to my wife, who keeps bringing home a dozen doughnuts? She can control herself to one a day. As for me, if a box of doughnuts is around, I'll eat it all in one sitting."

He went on: "When I ask her not to buy doughnuts, she says I need more self-control, and I should know better because I'm a diabetic."

He completed a genogram. His response, when he had finished listing the addictive personalities of his family, was:

"So I'm stuck. My relatives were drunks and drug abusers, so I'll become one. That's why I have no self-control even with doughnuts—the gateway drug to vodka," he said, laughing.

"No. Many a teetotaler (a non-drinker) has two parents who were alcoholics," I answered. "Genetics don't make your life. You do."

A pound of knowledge is worth a pound of cure

A genogram allows you to understand how your community and family may affect you. Such knowledge can help you avoid landmines, or reveal strengths you can draw upon in time of illness. The negative traits of others do not inevitably become yours. Positive ones can be nurtured.

Many people harbor these family tendencies, and they allow bitterness (like the kind Mr. G felt towards his wife) to take over their thoughts, or they deny themselves the ability to enjoy today's good and healthful things. Others use their knowledge to draw upon in times of crisis.

Mr. G shared his genogram with his wife. His tendency to "overdo it" was familial. He revealed this trait not as an excuse for his lack of self control, but rather as an opportunity to ask for and receive help from his family in controlling his food impulses. Mrs. G agreed to bring home only one doughnut for each of them from then on.

Similarly, Claire and her daughter Larisse used techniques like these to restore their family's health. "At least we're talking without shouting," said a more hopeful Claire, whose physical health had also improved.

A family ceremony:

Dinner together and more table talk

What are the practical applications of the Second Pathway for us in today's communities and families? Modern families eat on the run. The traditional family dinner, a customary time for sharing, is eroding, which compromises its potential to build healing relationships. Even when we do sit together, my teenager pretends I'm the interrogator. I ask, "How's school?" but all I receive back is, "Okay."

It is hard to build a healing relationship with a monologue. You may ask, as I did, "Are teenagers' minds frozen inside? How do I draw them out?"

Don't worry about brain activity. It's there, all right. What's needed is another approach.

Other table talk

- *Discuss the family schedule for the next week. Let the kids go first. You might learn about their interests and friends: what and who they like to spend time with.*
- *Each family member gives another family member a compliment. Suggest the person they argue with the most, but don't tell them that's why you made that suggestion.*
- *Instead of giving advice, ask for a child's thoughts about a topic, such as where the family should go on vacation. ("What do you think ... ?")*

Ask your child to write a list of things he or she wishes to do in the next five years:

- *Places to visit.*
- *Things to do, such as start a sport, etc.*
- *Relatives to see or friends to visit who have moved away.*

PRACTICAL SUGGESTION: Try a talk teaser

Option one

Say something that's topical, or provocative, such as:

"I read in the paper (saw on TV, heard, etc.) that the city is putting a curfew on kids. What do kids at your school think?"

Or: "Experts think kids should sleep longer in the morning. What do you think?"

Usually teenagers have an opinion about any limits on their freedom or the personal effects of their sleep. You'll gain their attention, and also gain insights into how they think.

Option two

Try telling a story about a grandparent, funny or inspirational or whatever comes to mind.

Grandkids and grandparents share a special bond. Use the strength of that relationship to build healing partnerships. Remember the joke: "Why do grandparents get along so well with their grandchildren? Because they share a common enemy—parents!"

What about healing ceremonies and relationships?

What about ceremonies or traditions and health? Here's an interesting and personal one "invented" by one of my wife's patients. Each year he sends her flowers for saving his life from a near-fatal heart attack, and to commemorate twelve more months of following a heart-healthy regimen of diet and exercise. His story shows the power of relationships and ceremonies. He was a reluctant husband sent in by his spouse for a checkup, which is not uncommon. In most clinics eighty percent of the patients are women, who come in early and often because they understand the value of prevention. For men, prevention is an oil change. They will take their cars to the mechanic before they will see a doctor about coughing up blood or other serious symptoms.

Southern Arizona, where I live, has the highest rate of melanoma, a potentially fatal skin cancer, in the world. (We recently surpassed Queensland, Australia.) Each year I see half a dozen men with melanoma-like lesions. I ask them if they had noticed that the mole had grown bigger, oddly shaped, or variable in color. To a man they say: "My wife (or girlfriend) has been after me for years to get that mole looked at by a doctor."

The stubborn sex

Women often ask me how to convince their husbands to go to the doctor or to participate in prevention. Three strategies help:

The Superman Strategy:

> I don't have much luck with playing this role myself when I outline the personal benefits of not smoking. "Doc, you gotta croak from something," they say. But if I let them be the rescuer ("Passive smoke kills 3,000 kids a year. Do you have kids or grandkids?") suddenly, it's not for themselves, but for someone else that they do it.

The Competitive Strategy:

> Men are competitive. During an annual exam the first thing they want to know is their cholesterol level. I try to allow them

bragging rights: "Yours is better than eighty percent of males your age." Or I say, "If you follow this food plan" (notice I say "plan" because men think "blueprint," not "diet," because women do that) "you'll beat most males your age."

The Make Me Rich Strategy:

One male patient said, "You're like my wife, you both nag me about my smoking and my eating."

I responded, "I like patients like you. Smokers use eighty percent more health care than nonsmokers. You're helping me put my kids through school. Financially, I can't afford it if you quit smoking."

For a second I thought he was going to deck me, and then he burst out laughing. Later with help he quit smoking and told me how much money he made investing the funds he had been wasting on cigarettes.

"Doc, you'll have to find some other sucker!" he said proudly.

Another man who was trying to lose weight said, "The guys at the office say I can't do it."

"How much are they willing to bet?"

"They're usually good for ten bucks each. There are five of them."

"So you could win fifty bucks if you bet them you could lose twenty pounds over the next five months (a safe regimen is one pound a week)." They bet against him, and lost, and bet he couldn't go a year, and lost again.

A couples plan

For both men and women, the power of healing is accentuated when both partners are involved in each other's health. For example, studies on smoking cessation have demonstrated that if both members of a couple quit together they are far more likely to succeed.

Now let's follow a particular patient's encounter with the medical system, with reference to the four pathways:

Aaron: a history

Aaron is complaining of upper abdominal pain.

"Work is getting to me," he says as he points to his chest. He feels terrible. What he says is: "My wife sent me in … I don't usually see doctors."

North

The spirit runs through the body. The doctor listens to the wak'a, the message behind the words. It must be serious if he never sees a doctor.

East

The power of relationships. Aaron's wife cares enough about his health to urge him to see the doctor.

West

Healing partnership with a healer. Not only does he feel horrible, but he looks it. His face is ashen and covered with profuse sweat, although his EKG (electrocardiogram, which measures the electrical impulses of the heart) is normal. His doctor looks beyond the test at the person, and calls 911 for the paramedics to transport him to the emergency room with a direct admission to the hospital.

"But we never do that!" the internist in the clinic tells his doctor.

Fortunately, his doctor is able to see past the test and the nay-saying colleague to the individual in need of help. Three hours later, Aaron undergoes emergency quadruple bypass surgery and lives.

Restoring healing balance. Other healing partners in his recovery include his cardiac rehabilitation team and a nutritionist who works with him and his wife to follow a heart-healthy diet.

South

The healing life cycle. Aaron has since changed to a less stressful job and takes problems at work less seriously. "Harmony" is his favorite description of his renewed life, which he celebrates each year with a gift of flowers to his doctor, my wife.

Roots and root causes: health partnerships

I shared Aaron's story with a Native healer. Her reaction was that Aaron wasn't working with his people, his family, and his community. What is striking in conversations with Native healers is that they do not see individuals as isolated objects or passive recipients, but rather as members of a group who must all participate to restore inner harmony and achieve recovery.

Not Alone

We are not alone.
The spirits of those gone before guide
our steps, our traditions, our beliefs.

We are not alone.
The care of those around us leads us
to healing and wholeness and comfort.

We are not alone.

—Mohawk/Onondaga healer

For example, as part of our community assessment class in the College of Public Health at the University of Arizona, we ask our graduate students: "How can you tell if a community is healthy?" What would you say if asked this question? Students from a Western industrialized background usually answer by suggesting analysis of:

- Hospitals
- Nurses
- Doctors
- Laboratories
- Disease rates
- Accident rates

However, our Native American students in the same class smile politely and consistently say that an unhealthy community will exhibit:

- Lack of inner harmony
- Disconnection from its traditions and culture

One White student challenged a female Navajo student to explain how fetal alcohol syndrome (a condition affecting babies whose mothers drank during pregnancy) would be solved by more harmony on the reservation. The Navajo student responded that alcohol was largely absent from her culture until the White man sold it. If a Navajo woman were in touch with her traditions she would never drink in the first place, the Native American student added.

And in support of her point, research by the Centers for Disease Control and Prevention indicates that at least half of all premature deaths in adults are caused by bad behaviors: overeating, alcohol and drug abuse, tobacco use, and sexual license. All of these may be seen as the results of a lack of inner harmony and lack of connection with a supportive community. The Navajo student believed the dominant White culture was focusing on symptoms and enumerating the fatalities, while her people were aiming at the root causes. At a traditional Indian medicine conference I attended in September of 2001, Taylor McKenzie, M.D., Vice President of the Navajo Nation, summed up the benefits of looking at underlying causes: "Psychosomatic conditions are where traditional Indian medicine excels." Native healers very effectively look beyond the physical symptoms of these conditions and sort out the underlying psychological causes.

Finding the way to harmony

The road to harmony is made easier by following the sacred pathways.

North:

Holism helps because the spirit is connected to the body.

East:

When it comes to healing, "one is the loneliest number." Health is more likely to be sustained in a partnership with family and community.

West:

Healing partners can guide the way.

South:

Ceremonies and practices such as the Navajo Blessing Way call forth healing forces for those who participate. Even a simple family tradition can help.

"They give my father a pill for chest pain. Sometimes it helps. Isn't that too late? Shouldn't they look for what causes the pain to start? The doctors are like a farmer who waits until he is starving before he decides to plant some seeds."
— Daughter of a Hopi patient

Finding the power of ceremony

What is the point and power of ceremonies such as sweat lodges and other similar activities? Annie the Navajo healer insists they remove obstructions, but I used to be a skeptic. "Never trust anyone over thirty," went the baby-boomer saying. Ceremonies, rituals, and traditions were equally disrespected by my generation. I even skipped my Dartmouth and Harvard graduations. (In both cases, I used those precious days between the end of classes and the next life commitment to take a trip with a brother.)

It took some time before I realized the power of the rituals all around me. Ever notice how people gravitate to the same seat each day in class or at a conference? A clergyman confided to me that he can readily "take attendance" at his services because most congregants choose the same seat week after week—and if the pattern is the same, it is easier to note who is missing. Breaks in patterns can be disturbing. Once as an experiment while I was a student I tried sitting in a different seat during every classroom lecture for just one week. Those around me seemed uncomfortable, and the students with whom I usually sat wondered what they had done wrong!

Rituals of life

How did many of us know that things were returning to normal after September 11? Our friends and family and business associates returned to the "ritual" of flying again.

Rituals fill our lives: how we eat, where we sit, when we awaken, what routes we take to work, whether we start shopping on the right or the left side of the grocery store, and on and on. Ceremonies are merely a form of ritual. For some, being ill is a ritual. Wake up and ache, carefully prop yourself up and take a pill, etc., etc. One great power in ceremony is to provide to those in need of healing a positive set of rituals, in place of negative ones. I have often found that a person remains stuck in an illness and a set of self-destructive "rituals" until he or she is given a ceremony that substitutes healing rituals for the "sick" ones. The ceremony serves as the spark for a warming fire that melts away the bad and reveals the better. These healing rituals and ceremonies can be short, such as taking a daily walk or writing a letter, or more involved, such as a sweat lodge or the nine-day Night Way of the Navajo.

"A ceremony for the person with an illness calms them, they feel less pain, their symptoms settle down. Their mind goes into the light, into another place. If they can do this, they feel better."
—Native healer

From negative to positive rituals

I see many patients with repetitive injuries from work or home activities. Several have had surgery for conditions such as carpal tunnel syndrome by the time they visit me (carpal tunnel is pressure on the median nerve in your wrist that can cause numbness and loss of strength). Negative rituals are often the cause of their condition.

Jed, a financial worker, complained that his hands always went numb from all the data entry he did during the last few days of the month. We confirmed that he had an ergonomically correct work station and that he lacked other medical conditions that can cause numbness, like diabetes, old injuries such as fractures, thyroid disorders, and so forth. When I asked why Jed couldn't divide up the work over several days, thus decreasing the intensity of the workload and the risk of trauma to his arms, his response was: "But I've always done it during the last two days of the month!" He had created a negative ritual.

Jed altered that injury-prone ritual to a positive one of spreading the data input to thirty minutes a day over many days. He needed a precise time, a ceremony, to make it a new work ritual; other people are less rigid in their requirements. The complex Indian ceremony? I wrote Jed's new routine down on a standard "work release" form available in every clinic.

Our Ceremonies

America claims it is a land that left ceremony behind.
No kings are crowned here on the backs of peasants,
And tradition is discarded as the dead ceremony of the living.
But we traditionalists know
Our ceremonies are our strength that sustains us.
The birthing of a new child,
The wedding of husband and wife,
The teaching of the wise elder,
The healing of those ill in body and mind.

These and more are our ceremonies.
They were our strength when everything was taken away,

They will renew us in hard times ahead.
They make us strong.
They are our strength.

—Cherokee healer

Ceremonies old and new

The power of relationships is never more evident than at ceremonies: weddings, confirmations, quinceañeras (a quinceañera is a coming-out party for young Hispanic women who reach fifteen), bar or bat mitzvahs, graduations, lighting weekly Sabbath or annual Advent candles, or any special event—even getting the car keys for the first time. Ceremonies don't have to be elaborate or expensive, though sometimes they are. A friend did complain that there was more "bar" than mitzvah in his son's ceremony after he saw the catering bill. In contrast, Apache lads used to demonstrate their manly prowess in a ceremony that only required a run and a mouthful of water. They would take a swig of water, run an Indian mile, and spit it all out at the end. My paternal grandfather would greet the New Year by taking a bag of groceries outside and coming through the front door—he was celebrating the Scottish Celtic ceremony of Hogmanay.

Smokers who quit often have colorful ceremonies. Harry, an enthusiastic ex-smoker, burned a dollar bill every time he wanted to light up (don't tell the U.S. Treasury). His reason: "It reminded me of how much I was wasting on cancer-causing leaves, my drapery and dry cleaning bill to get the stink of tobacco out of my house, and what I saved on life insurance and health care."

A dieter named Jackie rewarded herself for every pound lost with a Tootsie Roll, her favorite candy. Candy and weight loss? Yes, but Jackie would try to eat the Tootsie Roll as slowly as possible, first smelling its aroma through the wrapper, then slowly unwrapping it, then savoring every wonderful chocolatey morsel. And then not eating another one until another pound vanished. The advantages? It's easier to make small changes than big ones. If she had to completely quit all sweets for months, she knew she would never do it. By giving herself a reward, combined with realistic small goals of only one pound, and not overdoing it, Jackie was more likely to succeed.

Ceremonies can be shared and ought to be passed on if possible, even by anti-ceremony boomers like myself. Or they can be created as they are needed.

PRACTICAL SUGGESTION: Create your own ceremonies

First try writing down traditions and ceremonies in your own life. These might include graduations, baptisms, naming ceremonies, quinceañeras, bar or bat mitzvahs, confirmations, promotions, retirements, or anniversaries. Other examples might be:

- Gift giving
- Making homemade gifts
- Naming of a child
- Spreading ashes of the deceased
- Fasting: Mormons have a fast Sunday every month; Jews fast on Yom Kippur.
- Cooking holiday recipes: Our neighbors in Southern Arizona had a family tradition of producing holiday tamales. Buckets of fresh white corn were husked, processed, and turned into tamales by the entire family, with lots of laughter and sharing.

Now what are yours?

1.

2.

3.

4.

5.

How about ones you would like to add?

1.

2.

3.

4.

5.

Make your own ceremony with others

"But I don't speak Navajo, I can't sing, and I feel ridiculous whistling. What can I do?" Make your own ceremony. We have one in my house: When I'm finished writing a book, my wife stops wearing black for her "deceased," long-absent husband. (Just kidding.) Elaborate preparations or expensive items are not essential. At the last Native healing ceremony I attended, the leader had a hole in his shirt and used old pickle jars to hold herbs. Examples of small personal ceremonies are:

- Take a walk in the park with the kids. Drop leaves in the creek, watch them pass under the bridge, and count how long it takes for them to reappear.
- Light candles each week on the Sabbath.
- Buy or make a new ornament for the Christmas tree every year. Better still, have it represent something memorable: a vacation, a new birth, a wedding.
- Make even diets count. When you reach your target, have a cookie (or a Tootsie Roll, like Jackie). Try eating just one slowly, savoring every morsel, instead of hogging down half a dozen before really tasting one.

A tradition of service, or everybody needs an Oneida

Jerome is one of only nine Oneida (one of the six Iroquois tribes) who live in my county. I met him at a plant nursery where he works to support himself through college. Jerome is tanned and tall, with a narrow hatchet-like nose, dark blue eyes, and a ten-kilowatt smile. He looks like the wartime photo (the first photograph he ever had taken!) of my grandfather, who as a teenager left the farm in the Mohawk Valley to enlist during World War I. Jerome's sweatshirt said, "Intertribal Youth Council." He told me the group was composed of other young Indians who did voluntary service for the nearby Tohono O'odham tribe, cleaning up yards, repairing broken windows, and doing other needed tasks.

"The Tohono O'odham aren't your tribe. Why do you help?" I asked.

His answer revealed a great deal. "When we help others, we help ourselves. It's not good to get too focused on your own problems, especially when others need more than you."

Self-absorption can lead to unhealthy mental conditions. Contributing to the well-being of others is an antidote to many life problems. Here are some suggestions on how to get started.

Firehouse Recipes Program

My favorite example of successful group work and partnering for better health is our Firehouse Recipes program in Tucson, Arizona. Firefighters cook and eat together. Each chef is a fellow firefighter who is chosen for his or her ability to produce flavorful, but often unhealthful, meals. How were we to convince firefighters with cholesterol problems (low good cholesterol, or HDL; high bad cholesterol, or LDL) to change their eating habits? To sell the program we had to be careful to include the firefighters' ideas, and it was imperative that the result not be branded as a "where's the flavor?" disaster.

Most firehouses, like many families, predictably serve eight to ten favorite dinners. The "health partnering community," which we defined as two or more people working together to effect positive change—in this case, firefighters—collected their top ten recipes. We had a nutritionist analyze their content and make substitution recommendations, such as canola oil for lard. With the Firehouse Recipes program in place, blood cholesterols improved, as did awareness of heart health in general.

Substitution suggestions

(Consult a nutritionist or doctor for more details, and if you have a medical condition.)

AVOID	SUBSTITUTE
Butter in baking	Applesauce
Milk Group Whole milk in any form, condensed milk, chocolate milk, cream, ice cream, ice milk sherbets, whole milk yogurt	**Milk Group** Three cups of skim milk, powdered skim milk, evaporated skim milk, low-fat buttermilk, skim-milk yogurt
Meat Group Fried meats, kidneys, liver, brains, sweetbreads, shrimp, caviar, mackerel, any fish canned in oil, corned beef brisket, spareribs, port butt, sausage, luncheon meats, frankfurters, bacon, duck, goose, and skins of chicken and turkey	**Meat Group** Six ounces of skinned chicken or turkey, cod, haddock, halibut, clams, crab, lobster, oysters, scallops, perch, water-packed tuna or salmon; limit lean beef, veal, lamb and pork chops, and ham to three ounces, three times per week
Dairy Group All whole milk cheeses (hard and soft) including cream cheese	**Dairy Group** Cheese—fat-free cottage cheese or cheeses from nonfat milk
Egg yolks	Eggs—no more than one a day, egg whites; low-cholesterol egg substitutes
Fruit Group Avocado (except as fat exchange)	**Fruit Group** Fresh, frozen, and canned fruit; juices and nectars
Vegetable Group None, except those creamed, fried, buttered, or au gratin	**Vegetable Group** All vegetables including potatoes Beans, omit if they cause discomfort

AVOID	SUBSTITUTE
Bread and Cereal Group Quick breads, rolls, pancakes, waffles, tortillas made with lard	**Bread and Cereal Group** All white or whole grain breads and crackers, all cereals, Melba toast, spaghetti, macaroni, rice, noodles, sweet potatoes, and potatoes
Miscellaneous	**Miscellaneous** Seasonings—salt, pepper, other seasonings and spices used in small amounts
Fats—all others, gravies, cream sauces, salad dressings	Fats—one serving equals amount listed: 1 tsp. butter, margarine, vegetable oils, shortenings, mayonnaise; 1 T. Italian or French dressing
Soups—all others	Soups—fat-free broths and those made from the foods allowed: soups made from skim milk; bouillon cubes or powder
Desserts and sweets—those made with fat, whole milk, cream, ice cream; nuts, coconut, chocolate, all other cookies	Desserts and sweets—ices, sherbet, gelatin desserts, fruit whips, cornstarch puddings made with skim milk, arrowroot cookies, cornflake macaroons, angel food cake, jellies and jams, honey, syrup, hard candies, frostings without fat, marshmallows, gumdrops
Beverages—all beverages made with chocolate, ice cream, whole milk, cream, or eggs	Beverages—coffee (regular or decaffeinated), tea, Postum, milk, carbonated beverages, fruit drinks and punches, skim milk, drinks made with skim milk, cocoa

Condition A: Where are we?	Condition B: Where do we want to be?
I just can't lose weight.	Keep moving. It's hard to keep weight on if you're in motion.
I know I need to exercise, but I don't like it.	Forget exercise. Be active with a neighborhood walking group, etc.
I keep focusing on my own problems.	Focus on a pink ribbon (for breast cancer) or anything that reminds us of others who are worse off. Volunteer.

"Alone we can do little; together we can do so much."

— Helen Keller (1880-1968)

Moving to West

A transition from condition A to condition B is easier with community support and participation in a group. While I was working with the Hopi, I asked if their sacred Katsinam were dolls or deities. "They convey our personal prayers to our gods for rain or good crops," was the answer. Native and other healers can facilitate or hinder healing, just as the rain can help or flood. And when the doctor/healer incorporates the person to be healed as an equal partner, not as a subservient person who receives commands, then healing flourishes. A good contemporary example of this is the Recovery Together program.

Resources

Baines, B K. The ethical will resource kit. Minneapolis (MN): Josaba, Ltd.;1998.

Burke V et al. Health promotion in couples adapting to a shared lifestyle. Health Educ Res 1999; 14:269-88.

Goodwin, P J et al. The effect of group psychosocial support on survival in metastatic breast cancer. New England Journal of Medicine 2001 December 13; 345 (24) 1719-1726.

10

Physician, Heal Thyself: a history

No one becomes evil at once.
—Juvenal (c. 60-140)

The hotel corridor was silent and gloomy. Most of the participants in the medical conference were already downstairs, but Celestina needed to find the occupant of Room 33, who was going to be late for his speech. A queue of plates of half-consumed food smeared with catsup littered the entrance like garbage scows waiting to unload. It was definitely Dr. Peter Drum's hotel room, thought Celestina.

Why did North Americans bury the taste of good food in the vinegary red chemical paste of industrially grown tomatoes? But then for them, eating was not a pastime to be shared and savored, as it was with her people in Peru (on the days when there was enough food to elevate eating above mere survival). Instead it was a compulsive fueling for other activities. Peter even sometimes justified his own consumption of the red paste by saying it contained healthy lycophens that prevented prostate cancer. Little things about the North astounded her still: liquid diets, a new tablecloth after each patron in restaurants, and food consumed while standing, even while driving. *¡Loco!* Craziness.

She rapped the paneled hotel room door with a peremptory knock and waited. Peter Drum was not a morning person. It would take several minutes for the limbus area of his brain to register, record, and send movement signals down neurons to his dormant body. Watching Peter wake was like waiting for a cat to clean itself. She realized she had spent much of her adult life waiting for Peter Drum. Now his audience, too, was waiting downstairs. One more knock, and she would leave.

"Go away," he said. She pounded again. Inside Room 33, Peter Drum pulled two pillows tight around his ears like a boxer using gloves to protect his head in a close round. What was that other sound ... an alarm of angry bees locked out of their hive? Peter log-rolled across the bed towards the alarm clock. "Ow!" An empty fifth of generic whiskey poked him in his very hung-over forehead. The duty-free price tag was stuck to the sheet: $38 U.S. dollars, discounted to $27. He had vowed never to take a bottle to bed again and felt disgust at his failing self-control. He would restart Alcoholics Anonymous again, even if he resented the thinly disguised religiosity and slogans like "One day at a time."

How long had the alarm been on? The clock read 11:26 A.M., which meant he had four minutes to his speech time. He slapped the buzzer button off, careful not to hit the adjacent portable computer, a laptop with CD-ROM and the entire Library of Congress on micro hard drive. A careless mistake last month had dissolved a 40,000-word consulting report into irretrievable electrons.

A persistent hard knock on the door irritated Peter, as loud to his alcohol-pickled brain as kettledrums. "Maid service? Leave some extra towels this time . . . and ice!" he shouted.

Celestina opened the door and entered. The room smelled of liquor. She never liked drunkenness, especially after her father destroyed himself on Pisco sours, the national drink of Peru.

"You always leave your door unlocked?" she asked, frowning.

"Huh," said Peter. The familiar hard-edged female voice covering a perplexing sweetness roused him. It was Celestina. "Nothing worth stealing after you left me," he said, sliding the bottle under the blanket.

"Get dressed. You're on in a couple of minutes." She lobbed a brown shoe at his head.

"Hey! I'm up . . . Toss me the other one." He threw the sheets off and stood up shoeless, but fully dressed in day-old clothes.

"When we lived together you never wore any clothes to bed."

"Gives me more time to prepare my speeches," Peter said, pulling on the shoes. He yanked up the socks rolled down to his ankles like bracelets and with both palms persuaded his hair to lie flat. The whiskey bottle clattered to the floor.

Celestina wrinkled her nose. "How can you live like this?"

"Live when I'm dead inside?"

"Peter, it wasn't your fault that Claire died," Celestina said. "We need a long talk someday, when there's more time."

"Someday! What about returning my calls?" He imitated her answering machine while he knotted a well-creased necktie. " 'This is the household of Celestina Madril and Richard Darlington, well known jerk . . . ' I wish I'd never introduced you two in Africa. Hand me those cufflinks."

"That's over." She picked up the Bolivian silver cufflinks from the dresser, her gift to Peter on his thirtieth birthday a decade ago, and tossed them underhanded. She and Peter had been Volags, medical volunteers in the Ethiopian refugee camps during the droughts of the 1990s, and Richard Darlington was one of a parade of camp visitors. Peter and Celestina had split up shortly after Claire died at birth and Peter's drinking accelerated. "Peter, there's something I must tell you. I've wanted to talk to you about Claire—"

The telephone rang loudly.

"Hang on." He cradled the phone. "Yes, that's right, a copy of all 58,000 names to each of the panelists . . . and Dr. Madril . . . yes, she's right here. We'll be right down. We're just getting dressed," he said, winking wickedly.

She threw a pillow at him in anger. He dodged and hung up the phone.

"Can you give me two endorphin pills?" he implored, ignoring her previous uncompleted sentence about Claire. "My head is splitting."

"You're a physician, prescribe them yourself," she retorted.

Didn't she know his medical license had been revoked? But maybe she had been away so long on international assignments that she hadn't heard.

Celestina sighed and offered three yellow scored tablets from her purse. "Peter, you never took medicine for headaches before."

"The drinking has activated my hepatic enzymes. I metabolize pain relievers faster." He swallowed the drug tablets without water.

"So you can't take pain." Well, you can sure give it, she thought. "Why don't you get some help? I left you Dr. Levitt's number."

Then she really hadn't heard about his lifted license and his mandatory meeting with Dr. Levitt, director of the state program for professional rehabilitation (nicknamed "the druggie doctor" by Peter's AA sponsor) and chairman of the New Babylon Psychology and Addiction department.

"Is that who you and your latest saw for couples counseling?" Brutal honesty was a Drum trademark.

"I said that's over. Goodbye, Peter." She wheeled away. Another unfinished conversation with Peter, another Peter Drum trademark. Once she had written a poem about him and called it "The Dark Side."

His face is that of a dead man
White as if no blood ran through his veins
His mouth lies straight as a line
With a nose so sharp it could cut your soul.
His black soulless eyes
Haunt you through a lifetime if you get one glance
That is what I thought the devil looked like
But now I know he can have the face of you or me.
Now I know.

"See me to the conference hall," Peter pleaded now, turning on his charm, "or I'll never find it in time."

She stopped. "Fine," she said summarily.

They walked in uncomfortable silence.

"*¡Buenos días!*" said the elevator operator, smiling openly.

"I'll take the stairs." Celestina started to turn away, but Peter pulled on her sleeve like a boy with his mother at a toy store, and they entered the elevator.

"Doctor Pedro!" The elevator attendant offered an open flask.

Peter Drum made no pretensions to high status, as Celestina had discovered early in their dating life. When he had an office staff, everyone including the janitor was invited to social gatherings. "I used to have his job," he said. At first she found his American egalitarianism unsettling, later refreshing, but today it was exasperating.

"Peter, only you could make drinking buddies in an elevator," she said with resignation. The trio descended to ground level. Peter gave the elevator man a ten-dollar tip. Peter and Celestina scurried to the Conference Hall, their footsteps clicking out a cadence.

"Turn here?"

"Next corridor," she said, pointing. "That's the marine ecology section talks. Abdi Nur has a virus that sucks up carbon dioxide—might control global warming."

"Brilliant idea," said Peter sarcastically.

"What's the catch?" she asked as they turned left.

"Too much virus and all the carbon dioxide is gone, so we turn into Mars. Too little, we get Venus. That's what they call putting all your money on red."

Celestina looked confused.

"Gambling it all on one chance in roulette," he explained.

"It's like another of your expressions," she said with amusement. "Putting all your birds in one basket."

"It's eggs in one basket."

"Do birds hatch from anything else?"

They laughed together.

She could fall in love with that laugh again.

A note on this history

Dr. Drum has all the characteristics of the healer in trouble, regardless of ethnicity, education, or title. Such healers often maintain their professional competency at the expense of their home or personal life. Eventually everything crumbles, as in this case with the loss of a medical license. They are usually sociable and make friends easily, even with the elevator attendant. They can be skilled at recognizing addictions in others, but blind to their own adverse behavior. Worse, they might acknowledge their addiction, but falsely believe that they, because of their superior talent or intellect, can overcome it at any time without help.

11

West: the third pathway

Restoring healing balance — Native healers

Treatment of the part should never be attempted without treatment of the whole. That is the error of our day, separation of the body from the soul.

—Aristotle (384-322 B.C.)

How do Native healers foster healing partnerships and patient-centered care? This chapter explains some of their essential techniques.

Look in the Yellow Pages under "Native Healers," and you will draw a blank. They do not advertise; they are not in competition with anyone. Most avoid public notice. "We live in the cracks," said one healer to me, explaining their relative obscurity. The majority of healers quoted in this book preferred to remain anonymous. Their philosophy in life is not to compete for market share or notoriety, but rather to live and work together.

After reading this section or pathway you will know how Native healers:

- Choose widely and wisely from Native and Western medicine
- Promote healthful living, balance, and purification in a connected world
- Use blessings, sings, and chants

And you will know how to use these practical methods to develop healing habits in yourself.

A clash of cultures ... or beautiful music?

When the Whites came to the Americas they offered beads for land, hoping to own more of it than anyone else. The Indians gladly accepted because only God could own the land, not man. So it is with life and healing. No Native healer will rush to the United States Patent and Trademark Office to register

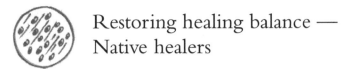

	NORTH	EAST	WEST	SOUTH
	Sun Duality of light (wave & particle) and humans	Wind Sacredness of words	Rain Life-giving	Earth
ACTION	*Know* Spirit runs through the body	*Understand* Power of relationships	*Build* Healing partnerships	*Create* Harmony with life cycle space/place
DESCRIPTION	Holistic approach Humans are more than a list of physical complaints	Group therapy Group support *No man is an island.*	Doctor-patient relationship Patient-centered care	Self actualization Homeostasis
NATIVE WORDS	Wak'a Care for/treat the soul	Talking stick, Talking circle Words of all heard with respect	Katsinam Convey individual comments/prayers to gods	Hozho Place of beauty (inner harmony)
ICON	Sun	Sweat lodge	Katsina	Sand painting
PATIENT ENCOUNTER	Doctor listens at a deeper level	Understands context of patient's family and community	Patient is center of healing, not to *do* to, but to heal *with*	Convert illness to harmony
EXAMPLE	Male with low back pain, won't go to work. Tests normal.	Wife with cocaine habit. He must stay home.	He could have gone to work, lost wife. Instead she joins Cocaine Anonymous.	He joins co-dependent group. He returns to work.
THERAPEUTICS	Discover true cause of illness	Engage family and co-workers	Develop synergy with patient	Restore natural life cycle

his or her "newest" drug. Their remedies are ancient and part of the public domain, or if they are secret they will stay that way without a patent.

Each of the 561 Indian nations in North America has something to offer, as does Western medicine. In my work I rarely hear claims of the superiority of one over the other. Native healing has been compared to an orchestra comprising different instruments and many sounds, which under the direction of the conductor and the composer make beautiful music together. Healing, too, is a partnership, not a race. No musician rushes to finish first (and if he does, he ought to keep his day job!) In concert the musicians are better and stronger, and so are healers and patients. Native healers also believe those to be healed, like the musicians, are more than physical beings. They are the spirit behind the noise or the sound waves, the spirit behind the body.

Good music and good healing each require composers, who gather knowledge, put it together, and hand it down, and conductors as well (Native healers or others), who can see the big picture and who can improvise, if necessary, by bringing in new pieces and instruments. Musical performances, like treatments, have their elements of ceremony: A conductor raises a baton; a Native healer might burn cedar and sage, use a prayer stick, or offer a treatment in a sweat lodge.

Pathways in the healer-patient partnership

North: ***Spirit runs through the body***

East: ***Power of relationships***

West: ***Build healing partnerships***

Take what you hear or learn from listening to the patient and the family, put it within the context of the community, and use patient-centered care. Tobacco smoking offers a common example.

Smoking kills, but how to stop?

"I can't quit smoking. I'm stressed at my job," complained my patient Bob, a nervous manager, after a recent promotion. "I'm embarrassed. I'm supposed to be an example of wellness for our younger staff (wellness is part of a mandated program for all workers) and for my kids. I'm a pariah at home. That's why I never smoke at home or let my kids see me doing it."

If we analyze his comments using the four pathways we see many ways to proceed.

- North: Listen to the wak'a, the voice within that speaks of anguish about his addiction.
- East: Involve communities in his recovery—his family and his work community.
- West: Build a healer-patient relationship.

The relationship with Bob developed step by step. First I offered empathy.

"This is a tough time for you," I said.

Empower, I reminded myself; don't overcome. "What about smoking is under your control?" I asked.

It's important to avoid coercion. Patients are ambivalent; they want to change, but another part of them seeks to continue the bad health habit. Why focus on behavior? The real reason many people die is due to their own behavior.

"What do you enjoy about smoking?" I asked Bob, continuing to gather information.

"I can leave my office and think," he answered. (He went outside for a smoke.) "I've quit before," he said. "I know I can do it."

I mentioned the benefits of quitting. "What do you stand to lose if you quit?" I asked.

Bob's answer was ironic. "Death, disability, loss of freedom if I get emphysema and have to use an oxygen tank. Smoking limits sports. Hurts appearance. No retirement if I die soon. Miss being a grandparent. I've thought about all of this," he added.

"Would it be useful to look at some information on quitting?" I offered.

Provide options, I thought. Avoid rushing, but offer help. "You can beat this disability; others have quit. I'd like to help you."

Support, support, support

It's important to provide support if a patient like Bob, a friend, or a family member fails to quit. Remember this great saying: "If you're not making mistakes, you're not alive!" I used to take these failures in my patients personally until I learned the average smoker quits three times before finally stopping.

Bob and I defined small increments or steps to success in stopping the behavior. One example might be buying nicotine gum. Other small increments we discussed were:

- Take mini-breaks more often, rather than one big break.
- Use stress busters such as those offered in Chapter 7.
- Medication: chew nicotine gum or wear a nicotine patch.
- Get up, go outside, look at a mountain view or the busy street, and imagine all the people lined up to see you dead at the age of sixty ... of a heart attack caused by cigarettes.
- Pretend you are on your deathbed and write your own obituary (see Chapter 5). Some topics to include:
    - These are the characteristics and events that made me what I am.
    - These are the experiences that influenced me the most.
    - These are the mistakes I made, and what I would change.
    - This is my definition of success.

Finally Bob and I chose a future time to discuss his behavior, his successes and failures, and to plan again.

But how should you choose wisely and determine if your healer is working in your best interest? Here is a sample case.

The burn-a-hole-in-your-stomach case

Mr. M, a relative of mine with an irritable stomach (described by his spouse as "an antacid junkie"), as well as rheumatoid arthritis that wasn't arrested by conventional treatments, traveled to Mexico to purchase an arthritis medicine that is notorious for irritating the stomach. At the same time, he was following the

Tobacco

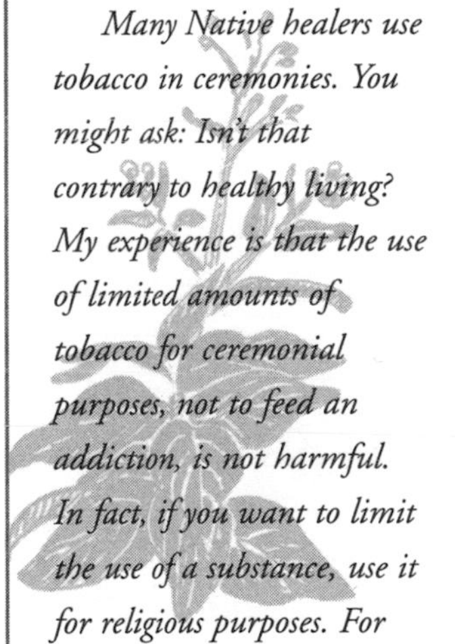

Many Native healers use tobacco in ceremonies. You might ask: Isn't that contrary to healthy living? My experience is that the use of limited amounts of tobacco for ceremonial purposes, not to feed an addiction, is not harmful. In fact, if you want to limit the use of a substance, use it for religious purposes. For this reason Indians have a lower rate of tobacco use than other groups, just as Jews who use alcohol for weekly Sabbath ceremonies have lower rates of alcoholism than the rest of the population.

Ancient trends in modern health

Many people already choose alternative medicine methods (See the discussion of alternative medicine and guidelines on herbs in Chapter 3.)

34% of adults used an alternative therapy in 1990
1 out of 2 used alternative therapy in 1997
425 million visits to alternative providers in 1990
625 million visits to alternative providers in 1997
(exceeds 388 million visits to primary care physicians)
$30 billion growth industry
75% of alternative therapies are paid for out of pocket (not covered by insurance)
This equals amounts spent on all hospitalizations each year in the U.S.A.

—Adapted from Eisenberg et al. New England Journal of Medicine, 1993

advice of another practitioner who told him to consume large amounts of highly acidic grapefruit juice. The combination of both stomach irritants sent Mr. M to the emergency room.

PRACTICAL SUGGESTION

A buyer's guide to alternative healing

Will it hurt other conditions?	Yes	No	Grapefruit contains acid that irritated stomach.
Will practitioner tell me what it is, along with its impurities and side effects?	Yes	No	Mr. M's Mexican doctor wouldn't label the ingredients.
Is the cost reasonable?	Yes	No	Mr. M paid $80 for indomethacin at the Mexican doctor's office. It retails for one third of that in the U.S.
Is there reliable literature to support its use?	Yes	No	Grapefruit juice is not a widely supported treatment for rheumatoid arthritis.

More skepticism

What can Native healers teach me? Look at how unhealthy American Indians are. Between 1990 and 1998 the prevalence of diagnosed diabetes in American Indians and Alaskan Natives aged fifteen to nineteen years old increased sixty-eight percent. These groups are 2.8 times more likely to have diabetes. Fifty percent of the Tohono O'odham, a tribe close to my home, suffer from Type 2 diabetes—the world's highest rate. However, non-Indians are also experiencing unhealthy trends, including a sixty percent obesity rate for American adults and thirty percent for children. Currently fifteen million Americans have diabetes.

Traditional since when? Or, coffee and a doughnut!

If you are on a reservation, ask about traditional Native American foods. The answers usually include fry bread, which is a dough of refined wheat flour fried in lard and covered with powdered sugar—in other words, a giant doughnut. All components are non-Indian foods and traditional only since the Indians were forced onto reservations and made to eat government-supplied flour, lard, sugar, and coffee.

Cut off from their genuine tradition of a mixed diet high in vegetables and fruits, berries, tubers, and occasional lean meats such as jackrabbit, Indians resorted to high-calorie, high-cholesterol foods. A modern, more sedentary lifestyle that leads to obesity also hurts.

Deadly genes

For most of the first 2.5 million years of mankind's existence, people didn't know if and/or when they would eat again. Famines were commonplace. (In ancient Scotland one meal every other day in winter was not uncommon.) To "pig out" was a survival strategy. Now it is killing us. Obesity accounts for 300,000 deaths a year in the United States, just behind tobacco as a cause of premature death. Native Peoples in particular possess a survival gene that helped them live through long famines. This "thrifty" gene increases the body's fat storage, a reservoir that can later be used during times of want—except that there are few wants today, and now the gene contributes to excess weight and its evil twin, diabetes. Native healers recognize this and are working to reverse these trends.

The dark side

There are charlatans and evildoers everywhere. Native healers are no exception. The Navajo call them Navajo Wolves or Skinwalkers, those who pursue evil at the expense of others. Perhaps you have heard some of the chilling stories of conventional medical professionals who have deliberately killed instead of healed? In his book *Demon Doctors,* Kenneth Iserson, M.D., details a number of these cases.

Others appeal to vulnerable people and to those susceptible to modern superstitions or "urban myths." The intent of these healers is not malignant, but they live outside the realm of the reasonable. One such individual convinced local residents that vaccines were a plot by the government to sterilize poor people. Actually the reverse is true. Mumps, a disease completely preventable by vaccination, causes sterility in many males.

Sialim tago Jiosh E-Tonalic O-Himetha.

O Creator, listen, forgive, and have mercy.

—Tohono O'odham prayer

Danger signs

Native healers as a rule are not licensed. Their activities are not monitored by an official governing body, though that is changing. The Veterans Administration now pays for certain healing practices, but not all, and it tracks results and healers. It is wise to observe these precautions:

- Bring a trusted companion, especially if you are female.
- Always ask for the contents and purity of any medicinal, botanical, or herbal remedy. See my introduction for websites and other sources of information.
- Question the need for repeated and frequent visits to a healer, especially if you aren't getting results. One healer offered a money-back guarantee if positive effects did not occur.
- Beware the healer who needs more healing than you. My intent is not to discourage healers to seek help, whether physical or psychological. But be cautious if healers don't seem to practice what they preach. How believable is a lung specialist who counsels others on the hazards of tobacco, but who is a chain-smoker?

Confidentiality or community? Privacy or isolation?

Finally, Native healers participate in talking circles and communal healing. What about confidentiality? Western medicine respects confidential medical treatment. So do traditional healers, but not at the risk of isolating those to be healed. Talking circles are but one example of a safe, protected place where you can avoid becoming isolated, and where the disease is not allowed to surround you. Sweat lodges are another. In such situations most of a patient's needs for confidentiality and privacy can be met while relieving him or her from the harmful isolation of illness.

Painting with sand

It is perhaps the Navajo who best demonstrate that healing is an art, something more than a craft, a profession, or a science. How curious, I thought at first, that Indians would paint with sand. How temporary! It would only take a slight wind to ruin the image. Stranger still, the painters do not wish their work to be recorded or photographed. This was not the world of Picasso or Chagall with reprints on every dorm room wall. Even more surprising was the use of sand paintings for healing. Medicinal plants I could understand. But a strange pattern on a dirt floor seemed unfathomable.

Holy ground

I learned that Navajo healers use sand paintings to represent their guiding deities or Yeis, the Holy Ones who lead the ill to wholeness and health. A crucifix or St. Christopher medallion serves something of the same purpose. But not really. Sand painters do not want their paintings reproduced because that way the images will lose their power, so these artists will alter an essential detail if they are compelled to sell their work commercially.

A Navajo healer at work on a painting is a study in patience. The colored stones (and other substances as well, including pollen and charcoal) are collected from special holy places such as Mirage Mountain. The healer spends hours grinding the stones into sand, practicing the designs that will best heal the patient, and finally crafting the image on the earth. It is that proximity to the soil that lends strength to the process. "Grounded" might be an English equivalent—literally.

Curiously, at the end of the healing ceremony the sand painting is erased. Why take all the trouble to create it? What a waste! Or so I thought until the next time I went to a typical Western wedding. The beautiful, billowy, expensive, fairy-tale-princess dress of the bride is usually worn but once. So it is with sand paintings. After a ceremonial singular use, they are stored away in the mind and memory of the recipient.

Some chanters and healers specialize in the Night Way, an elaborate Navajo sing or healing ceremony that can extend for as long as nine days. Whole teams may participate in its planning and completion. It is a winter ceremony that focuses often on people in the later years of their lives when arthritis and other disorders prevail. One experienced chanter will coordinate the sand painters in their design of the appropriate Yeis for the one-sung-over, the receiver of and partner in healing.

The value of sand

Each sand painter carefully weighs out the sand as if it were gold. Each color represents something divine and special. Watching sand painters at work, I remembered the European colonists on the East Coast who asked the Indians where all the gold was. And the Indians showed them yellow corn—more valuable to them than the metal because it was edible and could sustain life.

So the sand painter converts ordinary sand into something extraordinary and valuable. It is, after all, only ground gravel, but it makes a grand combination of colors, shapes, styles, and individualization for the one to be healed. The painter sings as he creates, which reminds me of my older relatives who did the same while working on the farm, shelling peas with a song on their lips. They almost made work glorious. So it is with the sand painter.

First he outlines the design with his finger, then with colored sand, and finally he fills in the shapes. The paintings have simplicity and order. A single image of a hand outstretched towards the sun speaks of a reconnection with the spirit inside. The person undergoing a healing shares in the creation. He or she becomes one with the chant, the picture, the symbolism, and the realization that this picture is uniquely crafted for them and will never be exactly duplicated for another. The intensity of attention and concern seems like a mother's hand on a fevered child's forehead. No chemical proof exists to demonstrate its efficacy, but the recipient is not concerned with science.

Multiple powers

And yet, there is research that strongly supports the power of the visual. Many people have a visual rather than an auditory learning style. Modern teaching methods feature multiple means of reaching students, and patients, for some learn better if they hear the material, others if they see it.

Biofeedback clearly provides the individual with a visual reading of the way biological functions are affected by the mind. Also, famous photographs demonstrate the impact of the visual. The photo of the young, naked Vietnamese girl burned by American napalm shocked a nation. And the picture of the firefighter holding the infant at the Oklahoma bombing is another image that conveys horror as much as or more than words.

Perhaps it is because Indian languages were unwritten until recently (Cherokee is an exception) that visual imagery is often employed in Native American culture. Of course their visual and oral past has not inhibited Indian writers such as N. Scott Momaday from receiving the Pulitzer Prize.

And now, with our expanded view of life, healers, and healing, we move towards the question of life sequences and transitions and their effect on health. But first we'll take a closer look at healing in action, hour by hour and day by day.

The Pollen Pathway

If gold is your hunger,
Let the yellow of honey sweeten your day,
Let the yellow of the sun grow the plants in your fields,
Let the amber of the corn feed your children,
Let the gold of the sunset warm your soul.
Follow the gold of the pollen way
And you will be happy with the all the riches that you have.

—Native Healer

Resources

American College of Sports Medicine Position Stand. Exercise and physical activity for older adults. Med Sci Sports Exerc 1998;30:992-1008.

Blair SN, Kohl HW 3rd, Paffenbarger RS Jr., Clark DG, Cooper KH, Gibbons LW. Physical fitness and all-cause mortality. A prospective study of healthy men and women. JAMA 1989;262:2395-401.

Courneya KS, Mackey JR, Jones LW. Coping with cancer: can exercise help? Phys Sportsmed 2000;28(5):49-73.

Iserson, K. Demon doctors: physicians as serial killers. Tucson (AZ): Galen Press;2002.

Jones DA, Ainsworth BE, Croft JB, Macera CA, Lloyd EE, Yusuf HR. Moderate leisure-time physical activity: who is meeting the public health recommendations? A national cross-sectional study. Arch Fam Med 1998;7:285-9.

King AC, Oman RF, Brassington GS, Blisise DL, Haskell WL. Moderate-intensity exercise and self-rated quality of sleep in older adults. a randomized controlled trial. JAMA 1997;2777:32-7.

Laurie, N. Healthy People 1020: setting the nation's public health agenda. Acad Med 2000;75:12-3.

Meredith CN, Frontera WR, O'Reilly KP, Evans WJ. Body composition in elderly men: effect of dietary modification during strength training. J Am Geriatric Soc. 1992;40:155-62.

Momaday NS. House made of dawn. New York: HarperCollins;1999.

Paffenbarger RS Jr., Hyde RT, Wing AL, Hsieh CC. Physical activity, all-cause mortality, and longevity of college alumni. N Engl J Med 1986;314:605-13.

Pate RR, Pratt M, Blair SN, Haskell WL, Macera CA, Bouchard C, et al. Physical activity and public health. A recommendation from the Centers for Disease Control and Prevention and the American College of Sports Medicine. JAMA 1995;273:402-7.

Robideaux, Y. UA Public Health News Fall 2001.

Shepard RJ. Exercise and aging: extending independence in older adults. Geriatrics 1993;48(5):61-4.

12

A Day in the Healing Life: a history

A man is what he thinks about all day.
—Ralph Waldo Emerson
(1803-1882)

5:30 a.m.

My first waking thought is: "Friday!"

The end of the week always brings me surprises. I believe people save up their best medical problems for the last regular workday. To be fair, maybe consciously or unconsciously they hope they'll have two weekend days to recover from whatever insults we inflict on them. My less charitable view is that some patients have a full weekend of activities and can't afford to be or remain sick; or maybe their employers won't let them see the doctor during work. Either way, the end of the day on Friday is their favorite time to visit me.

My morning starts with a run in the Sonoran desert that surrounds our house. Then I collect the eggs from our chickens. One belongs to a South American species that lays lime-green eggs, so we sometimes eat a Dr. Seuss breakfast of green eggs and ham. Next I write a few pages on my book in progress, get breakfast for the youngest child while my working spouse, also a physician, rouses the other two, and then I start dinner. I like Crock Pots because you can throw the ingredients into one in the morning (today it's a few potatoes, carrots, onion soup mix, stewed tomatoes, and diced chicken), and dinner's ready when you come home.

7:15 a.m.

Carpool begins. We have three children in three different schools, and I transport the two oldest and a neighbor child today.

7:45 a.m.

At the University of Arizona in Tucson, I work as an associate professor in both the College of Medicine and the College of Public Health, which means I teach as well as practice medicine. I rush to the mailbox before clinic, sort through the correspondence, and dump the junk mail in the trash.

8 a.m.

Review the specialists' reports, the MRI, CAT scan and X-ray results, and the laboratory tests of the dozen people I'll see today.

I have an ongoing health and wellness program for 800 individuals that includes health risk appraisal with an assessment of physical and psychological factors, such as:

- Stressors in their life
- Coping skills
- Relaxation techniques
- Hobbies
- Support systems
- Tobacco, alcohol, and other substances
- Physical activity, frequency, type, and duration
- Nutrition, type and variety of foods, and methods of preparation
- Preventive maintenance such as breast exams, dental flossing, etc.

We also measure their aerobic capacity, strength, grip, and flexibility, along with skin folds and body mass. We give electrocardiograms, take vital signs (blood pressure, pulse), and do back assessments. We test range of motion and vision, including peripheral vision testing, and we also do pulmonary (lung function) testing. But that's only the beginning of the tests.

Technical terms pile up fast: CBC, cardiac/lipid profile, HDL/LDL ratios, cholesterol, c-reactive protein, blood chemistry profile (SMAC), liver and kidney function, glucose, electrolytes, proteins, calcium, urinalysis with microscopic analysis.... We test for prostate and cervical cancer, and each year everyone also receives a complete physical examination. We review every measurement, and we give each participant a personalized/individual 25-page wellness-fitness report with recommendations for physical and mental well-being. And those with risk factors for heart disease get a treadmill test.

Whew! Where's all the Native healing, you ask? Every day I attempt to incorporate elements of the Four Sacred Paths into my discussion with patients, whenever appropriate. I also learn a great deal from my patients, and today is no exception.

8:30 a.m.

First patient arrives. Joanie, a thirty-year-old manager, has rheumatoid arthritis that began when she was an adolescent. I'm seeing her for pain related to typing; she needs an ergonomically correct workplace (I have published two books on that theme).

Joanie is doing well with her medications, but when she really hurts, she tells me, she fasts for a day, ingesting only water, and the pain completely vanishes! The only problem is that to stay pain-free Joanie would have to starve. Her best treatment is not found in any medical text or article, but it works. I remark that many societies promote fasting (Indians on certain occasions, Jews on Yom Kippur, Mormons on their monthly fast Sundays) for its spiritual and other benefits. We discuss Joanie's diet to see if there are any foods that might contribute to her condition (for example, painful joints may be related to another condition known as gout or high uric acid in the blood, attributed to diet and alcohol).

Joanie asks about the diet of the indigenous peoples of the Americas, since I mentioned Indians. I explain that their original diet was varied and nutritious. In fact, the diabetes that is rampant among American Indians was unknown before the white man arrived.

The Native diet was rich in variety and filled with disease-blocking vitamins and minerals and cancer-preventing antioxidants and fiber. Common elements included:

- Meats such as venison and wildfowl, which were low in fats and cholesterol. (The non-domesticated turkey provided to the Pilgrims in Massachusetts Bay Colony had little resemblance to the antibiotic-laced, obese bird on steroids we gorge on every Thanksgiving.)
- Fish like salmon, which were filled with heart disease-preventing Omega 3 (or "good") fats.
- Nuts and acorns, which contain protein and monounsaturates that are healthier than the saturated and trans fats so prevalent in the Western diet.
- Fruits such as berries and stone fruits.

- Vegetables grown above ground (squash, beans, milkweed, wild cucumbers, asparagus).
- Vegetables grown below ground (onions, potatoes, wild turnips, carrots).
- Grains such as corn.

In addition, foods were prepared more healthfully:

- Baked items were cooked without the dangerous saturated oils in use today.
- Meats, fish and vegetables were dried, broiled, boiled, or smoked.
- Less fat was used to cook foods, and none was added to those dried or boiled.
- Foods did not sit in fat.

Also Native Americans relied more heavily on safer vegetable sources of protein, instead of animal proteins that may be involved in causing colon, breast, and prostate cancer. The Inca even learned how to freeze-dry potatoes for later use. They would squeeze out the water and place the potatoes on their roofs so the freezing night air of the Andes would preserve them.

Importantly, the Native Peoples kept physically active hunting, farming, collecting, and preparing their foods. Rather than being indulged by television, they entertained themselves with movement, games, songs, and dances. Such physical activity is one of the best "medicines" of all for its benefits on every body system and its disease-preventing power. Lastly, the Indians always thanked the Creator for the food, and even the animal that gave its life that they might eat and be healthy. "Sheep are full of vegetables and therefore filled with medicine," says Annie, the Navajo healer.

10 a.m.

One by one, I see five more patients. Then I drive to the Gila River Indian Reservation near Phoenix for a meeting with tribal representatives from across the state of Arizona. They discuss their incorporation of traditional healing methods with Western techniques.

One tribal official meets with me privately about ways to encourage health careers among Native Peoples so that they can become self-reliant and not dependent on transient medical outsiders.

"The problem is that the government sends us outsiders," he says. "By the time they learn our ways their term of service is up, and we have to start all over again. It's like a drive-by shooting. Now you see them, now you don't!"

So they hope to further develop a cadre of Native doctors, nurses, pharmacists, and others who are more likely to stay on the reservations and who will be culturally competent in the ways of their people. (Many current health care providers are non-Indians who are completing a federal loan commitment and who will leave the reservations after a few years.)

4 p.m.

I make it back to the clinic (it's a three-hour round trip from Tucson to the Gila Reservation). A paramedic named Harold is here. He can't relax. He keeps replaying a bad event over and over again, ever since he went on a devastating call.

As a paramedic Harold has seen death many times, but this particular one tore him up—a code arrest of a young child. Everything that could possibly have been done was done; he ran the code arrest as well as anyone could, but the child died. And the dead boy was Harold's own son's age. The image of that child, then of his own, and finally of the child's stricken parents, has overcome him. Harold is tormented by a recurring nightmare of the death.

Usually it helps to keep busy. As my great-aunt Pearl used to say, "If you're busy you're happy." But busy for this paramedic means more code arrests, more kids, more reminders. He can't escape the trap in his own head, and his health is starting to suffer.

"What will become of me?" Harold says in despair. "I love what I do, but I can't go on like this. I can only sleep for three hours at a time when I'm home, and at work, with all the calls at the fire station, it's worse."

Our emergency medical system (EMS) professionals have seen it all during their careers, but some deaths are harder to bear than others, as was this one. Twenty years later I can still see the faces of the little ones who died in the refugee camp in Somalia where I served as a volunteer. Harold and I cover a lot of ground and come up with many methods to help him. Focusing only on Harold's physical symptoms would be inadequate. All four pathways will be needed to help him restore harmony to his life so he can return soon to the job he loves—serving the public.

The four healing paths encompass:

North

The spirit runs through the body — spirituality and healing

We discuss pastoral care. Harold is connected to a faith community and I urge him to speak with a member of the clergy. He belongs to a congregation that has a faith-based counseling program, so we arrange an appointment that same day.

East

The power of relationships — healing as a group activity

His spouse and children are supportive, and I include them in the recovery plan.

West

Restoring healing balance — Native healers

Harold is on track, connected, and in tune with all the elements of healing. We review natural and medicinal sleep aids. First I teach him a relaxation technique to put his mind at rest. Then I make certain that he doesn't have any adverse insomnia-producing habits or conditions like exercising before bed (which increases sleep-preventing catecholamines and raises the heart rate), use of caffeinated products, temperature fluctuations, external light, or noise disruptions in the bedroom.

South

The healing life cycle — beginnings and endings and the next world

Child deaths are the most difficult of all for health care and emergency staff. We see death regularly, but we feel we have let the world down if a young one dies under our care, even if it was unavoidable and not our fault as in this case. Harold's clergy member will provide him with spiritual reassurance during this difficult time, and I remind him of how many children he has rescued in the past.

"How many kids are alive today because of your efforts?" I ask.

So many, he says, that he can't begin to count them, and he has department commendations and grateful letters from numerous parents and grandparents to attest to his contributions. I tell him to keep his favorite letter in his pocket at all times. When doubts emerge I advise him to read it. (And to make a long story short, his personal and professional life eventually do return to normalcy.)

4:45 p.m.

I try to write a few lines for my book. I have always admired the great physician writer William Carlos Williams who composed poetry in between patient visits in his clinic in New Jersey. I don't think he did it with three children to transport and help with homework, a working spouse, or the interruptions of a pager or cell phone.

5:30 p.m.

I finish typing my chart notes and try to reach my daughter's school before they lock her up for the weekend! I return two calls on my pager: one from Harold's clergy member, and one from my co-instructor in the community assessment class we teach for public health professionals.

6 p.m.

Dinner is ready in the Crock Pot, and the other two children are home (thank God for carpools). My wife has the late shift at her work and will join us later. I hustle the oldest child out the door, as she needs a ride to a school event, and take the other two to a religious occasion.

As I drive west I see the setting sun bathe the cerulean southwestern sky with reddish-orange hues, and I feel grateful to be a part of this corner of the universe, and to have the opportunity to participate in so many lives, so many happenings. I recall the four Navajo principal elements, with gratitude for their presence:

The Sun that brings warmth
The Wind that brings the rain clouds
The Rain that gives life-giving moisture
The Earth that gives nourishment . . .

And at this point I try a visualization technique. I imagine what a relief it will be when at least one of the kids can drive!

13

South: the fourth pathway

The healing life cycle — beginnings, endings, and the next world

Breathe in the light of the new day, the dawn.
Give thanks for the new day for those around you, for life, for everything.
Then you will become whole again.

—Navajo healer

After reading this section you will understand:

1. How Native healers and their practices restore health, helping patients reach a state where mind, body, spirit, and community are in harmony with a natural life cycle, including:

   Childbirth and beginnings
   Grief and endings
   Space and place in health (hozho)

2. You will also understand how you can use practical suggestions and personal healing habits to maximize your healing and to incorporate healing partnerships in your own life.

Beginnings

The woman's scream ended in a gurgle. "The first child for a first-time mother is always born in fear," said Silvia as she cut the newborn boy's umbilical cord with a knife she had carefully boiled. She was proud of her skill as a healer and midwife, but something was wrong this time.

The woman screamed again. There was no time to bless or bury the placenta in Mother Earth. She pushed deep into the woman's belly. Another scream, only weaker. Then Silvia felt the head of a second child! It was not

	NORTH	EAST	WEST	SOUTH
	Sun Duality of light (wave & particle) and humans	Wind Sacredness of words	Rain Life-giving	Earth
ACTION	*Know* Spirit runs through the body	*Understand* Power of relationships	*Build* Healing partnerships	*Create* Harmony with life cycle space/place
DESCRIPTION	Holistic approach Humans are more than a list of physical complaints	Group therapy Group support *No man is an island.*	Doctor-patient relationship Patient-centered care	Self actualization Homeostasis
NATIVE WORDS	Wak'a Care for/treat the soul	Talking stick, Talking circle Words of all heard with respect	Katsinam Convey individual comments/prayers to gods	Hozho Place of beauty (inner harmony)
ICON	Sun	Sweat lodge	Katsina	Sand painting
PATIENT ENCOUNTER	Doctor listens at a deeper level	Understands context of patient's family and community	Patient is center of healing, not to *do* to, but to heal *with*	Convert illness to harmony
EXAMPLE	Male with low back pain, won't go to work. Tests normal.	Wife with cocaine habit. He must stay home.	He could have gone to work, lost wife. Instead she joins Cocaine Anonymous.	He joins co-dependent group. He returns to work.
THERAPEUTICS	Discover true cause of illness	Engage family and co-workers	Develop synergy with patient	Restore natural life cycle

moving down the birth canal. If she didn't work quickly, both of the babies would die. In the hard times past, one or both twins often died because the mother didn't have enough milk to feed them both.

Silvia was a descendant of a long line of healers. Her brown hands worked quickly. If she could only reach the baby's head, she could deliver this child. With her left hand, she pressed on the stomach, as her right hand reached into the woman's vagina. She could barely touch the second baby. The first child squeaked like a bird out of its nest, wanting his mother.

Then Silvia felt a baby's bottom with her right hand. That was the problem; the second baby wanted to feel the earth with its feet first instead of coming out head first like normal babies. Silvia chanted one of her people's prayers for new life. She had a good memory for such sayings, better than anyone but Shaman, her grandfather.

Again she pressed down on the woman's abdomen with her left hand, forcing the second baby into the pelvis. Silvia felt one foot. The baby kicked. She caught the other foot between her fingers but then lost it. Everything was slippery. Another kick, and she had both feet. She pulled ... a second boy, fortunately smaller than the first.

The Whites would cut open a woman's abdomen and remove babies, even if they could be delivered naturally and safely. And they said *her* people were "savages"!

Silvia cut the second umbilical cord, delivered the placenta and blessed it in the traditional way. She massaged the woman's belly as her mother had instructed her; it always seemed to slow down post-birth bleeding.

The two male newborns greeted the new morning with eyes blinking and tongues licking the air, searching for a breast. The rising sun rose in a shimmering glare of red, and hit Silvia's eyes like rivets as she dreamed of rain clouds that never seemed to come. Her secret name meant sunrise, but lately she wished only for darkness and shade. The area surrounding her was part of that great expanse of Southwest known as the Sonoran Desert. Silvia had little time for daydreams in these drought-filled days, but sometimes the sun and weariness, combined with too little food, caused her mind to wander. She often imagined a lush oasis, full of water, surrounded by trees, with many fat deer coming down to drink—all a desert mirage. A man of her people could survive three months without food before he starved to death. A woman, who had a higher percentage of fat, could last a little longer. A child, much less.

Too much nutrition

In the past her people had consistently suffered from too little nutrition. Now too much nutrition of the wrong foods caused new maladies such as diabetes. Among Southwestern Native Peoples diabetes was once unknown, but now they had the highest rates in the world; one in four Tohono O'odham had a family member on kidney dialysis. The reason? The so-called thrifty gene, which allowed them to hoard fat during times of plenty and efficiently use it during long months of famine, when combined with Western food habits, led to devastating diabetes.

For Native healers, wellness is restored when mind, body, spirit, and community are in harmony within a natural cycle. To help restore the natural cycle, Silvia prepares traditional foods such as prickly pear cactus pads or *nopales*, called *nopalitos* when small and edible, which contain a substance (mucopolysaccharides) that partially neutralizes the effects of diabetes. The fruit of this cactus (including various species of *Opuntia*) is also edible.

Other life supports: nursing

Breast-feeding has innumerable benefits for children: It promotes immunity to disease, nutrition, and cognitive development, and it decreases infections, especially those of the middle ear. Fathers can participate by introducing an occasional bottle early. Consult La Leche League or your health care provider for advice. Native cultures have, by necessity, encouraged breast-feeding. Because breast milk can transmit many substances from mother to newborn, caution is advised. My wife had to avoid spaghetti because the spices bothered our first-born.

Breast-feeding uses large amounts of fluid, so keep well hydrated with eight to ten ounces of water, fruit juices, or milk every waking hour. Stay away from alcoholic and caffeinated products. Some pregnancy symptoms such as cramping, headache, and fatigue can be early warning signs of dehydration. Just because you are urinating frequently doesn't mean you are well hydrated—the baby's head pressing on your bladder may be the cause of frequent toilet visits. Don't wait until you are thirsty. "Keep your 'pee pale,'" says Miriam, a Native midwife. Irritated breasts or nipples can be treated with poultices or emollients. Mastitis is an infection of the milk ducts and surrounding tissue, characterized by swelling and redness in the breast(s), and

Prickly pear recipes

Nopalitos (Cactus Pads)
Preparation: Use tongs to collect the young, tender pads. (Occasionally they may be purchased raw in vegetable markets.) Boil for fifteen minutes. Place on cutting board and scrape off stickers with a knife. Cut off base of pad and 1/8 inch around the pad's edge. Dice.

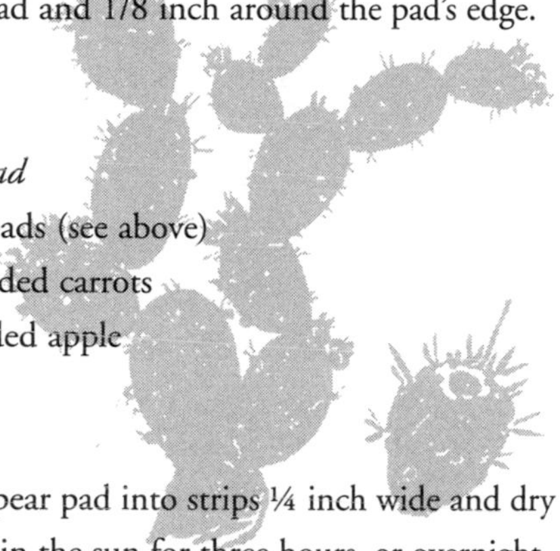

Nopalito Salad
2 prepared pads (see above)
2 cups shredded carrots
1 cup shredded apple
¼ cup milk

Cut prickly pear pad into strips ¼ inch wide and dry in a flat pan in the sun for three hours, or overnight, until strips are chewy. Chop into small pieces. In a bowl combine all ingredients
NOTE: Canned or frozen *nopalitos* are occasionally available from Latino food suppliers.

Prickly Pear Fruit Strips
Pick the prickly pear fruit with tongs, place them in a large plastic container, rinse, and freeze them. Then allow them to defrost. Press them with a potato masher and then pour the "purple mess" through a fine-mesh colander. Mix 4 cups of prickly pear juice with 4 teaspoons of honey and 6 ounces of grape juice or other fruit concentrate. Spread on a cookie sheet covered with plastic wrap. Dry in an oven at the lowest setting; this can take all day. After the fruit leather is dry, peel the plastic off, roll up in strips, and enjoy.

increased temperature. It usually occurs one to four weeks after delivery and is often due to a penicillin resistant staphylococcal infection. Antibiotics are usually indicated, but don't use tetracyclines as they can stain a newborn's developing teeth. Sulfonamides and nalidixic acid can cause red blood cells to break down in infants deficient in G6PD. All antibiotics can pass into a mother's milk and can potentially cause diarrhea, candida (yeast) infections, and allergic reactions in the infant. Breast-feeding may have to be suspended during some medication use. Consult your doctor.

Certain herbal products are used by Native healers for sore breasts and nipples. Because herbicides are ubiquitous and can pass through the milk to the child, I would caution readers not to use such products unless the producer can guarantee safety for the newborn. In the past, Native healers have used calendula tea (*Calendula officinalis*) to enhance breast milk output.

Childbirth and childhood

Among the Hopi a Katsina—a carved representation of an appropriate guiding spirit, such as Hahai-i Wuhti, "Pour Water Woman," or the Kachina Mother—is presented to the pregnant mother and also later to the newborn baby. In many tribes, such as the Mohawk, men participate in childbirth. Native Peoples often believe that "others," including the spirits of deceased relatives, are present during the birth process.

Childbirth is an experience full of duality for all concerned, including child, parents, family, community, and health practitioners. If all goes well, there is no experience more joyful. When it does not, the pain of a stillbirth, a damaged child, or an ill or dead mother is lasting and deep. The spirits are there to give life abundantly and to retrieve it reluctantly, if need be. In many Native cultures it is particularly important who is present at the birth. Among Canada's First Nations, invitees include those who ask to be there, the midwife, the person the child will be named after, and those who are "wise," in hopes that this trait will be transmitted to the newborn. Of course the best planning can go awry. The doctor for my mother's birth was too drunk to travel, I was delivered by a scared but handy hospital clerk, and one of my daughters almost arrived in the back seat of our car!

Community and connection

By tradition among the Pueblo Indians, to promote bonding, the newborn is cleaned, then wrapped in a soft blanket and held by the mother. The Inuit choose another child to befriend the new baby for life—an enduring birth buddy. The grandparent for whom the child is named also shares a special bond with the child throughout the Native child's life. Naming ceremonies might include the entire clan, whose members by their presence commit themselves to the nurture and well-being of the new child.

As human lives move through their cycles, in sickness and in health, we can gain strength from understanding and accepting where we stand in the larger pattern of existence. Connection to community is important for both older and younger generations. A recent family wedding in Canada drove home to me the importance of ceremony at transition stages. There are few times in modern life when three or four generations connect.

PRACTICAL SUGGESTION: Ideas to grow connections

- In weddings, include something from the grandparents. At one I attended, the groom read a love letter from his father to his mother. Although the words seemed old- fashioned, the obvious affection was moving. "Old" stuff can be evergreen and engaging for all involved.
- Another couple had the clergy person read the wedding vows of the groom's grandparents after the bride and groom exchanged more modern vows. This brief addition was heartwarming and appreciated by all: It connected past to present and underlined the fact that some things never change.
- Jewelry items are often handed down. A grandparent or parent's ring may be incorporated into the wedding ring of the newest generation.
- All or part of a relative's dress or bridal veil may be used by the new bride.
- Use your imagination. I've found the older person is usually flattered when the younger asks for ideas or a memento item to borrow.

Why does ceremony so permeate Native cultures?

I believe ceremonies work to maintain connectedness between the generations. Choose the occasion: child namings, confirmations, marriages, graduations, and funerals—all involve a ceremonial element. A common thread is the continuity of life from beginnings to joinings to endings. As much as we moderns try to dilute ceremony, it keeps re-emerging. I've been to many marriages where the old practice of "something old, something new, something borrowed, something blue" persists. In several cases the bride has taken great pride in the "old" being a piece of jewelry or other item from a beloved grandparent. (My wife's wedding ring contains two stones from her grandfather's cufflinks.)

The "grand" generations

There is a special bond between grandchildren and grandparents. Often parents will name children after a grandparent, and middle names are frequently borrowed from older relatives. Ashkenazi Jews often take the first letter of a name that belonged to a deceased family member and use it as the first letter for a child's first name. Sephardic Jews follow the same practice but with a living relative. A traditional Latin American's full name incorporates maternal and paternal sides with several generations listed.

How can this help with healthful living? The benefits are many, including a feeling of community, connection, and personal well-being, physical as well as mental and spiritual. Intergenerational ceremonies and activities promote:

- A sense of belonging
- A feeling of unconditional love
- A resource for support during times of physical or psychological need

PRACTICAL SUGGESTION: Grandparent-grandchild activities

Mail

A simple postcard from grandparent to grandchild (and the reverse) is an easy way to stay in touch. E-mail is another option, and many people now send digital photos to enhance the visual experience.

Hobbies, skills and hanging out

My colleague Carlos fondly remembers his grandfather taking him bird watching. He continues this hobby and the cross-generational practice to this day, and he recently took his first grandchild on a similar birding jaunt.

Don't have a hobby or skill to share?

Our friend Molly speaks of her sleepovers at Grandma's as one of the high points of her childhood. My nephews and nieces belong to a bowling team organized by my sister-in-law's mother.

Instant heirlooms

A transition such as a graduation or a wedding is a good time to take everyone's picture (you can group families) using rapid developing film. Paste the pictures in a scrapbook. Have everyone write a brief note to the graduate or the bride and groom next to his or her own picture. These intergenerational scrapbooks made at life's turning points are cherished for decades and become "instant" heirlooms.

An additional transition generational bonding tool is to take a picture of the graduate or the bride and groom and attach it to the middle of a frame that is large enough to allow others to write a comment on the border. An example: "Wishing you the wisdom of Solomon, the patience of Job, and the children of Israel." Or: "Marriage may be an institution, but it is never a reform school."

Funeral customs

Ask family members to bring favorite mementos or photos to the funeral ceremony or the reception. This "offering" connects the family and invited friends and guests. The photos help attendees recall happier times, and guests who may not have known the deceased, but who are present as a courtesy to one of the family, learn something interesting through the photographs. Check with the presiding clergy, as some are restrictive about these activities (or if you hire a funeral hall, you can do it your way.) After a funeral, it is common to hold a wake (be sure to assign designated drivers to prevent another funeral, if alcohol is used). Participants can take turns toasting the departed. In Latin America, All Saints' Day and All Souls' Day (November 1 and 2) provide an opportunity to reconnect with those who have passed on. Graves are decorated with food and flowers; carnations are a popular choice in border towns near my home. The American Memorial Day can be more than a day off work. It might be an occasion to visit a cemetery and take turns telling your best-loved story about deceased relatives and friends, or to go to their favorite restaurant and have a meal in their honor.

Sacred places

At midlife Jake's life was in shambles from a painful divorce, a job loss, and a persistent stabbing pain "like a screwdriver between my eyes." Although he was a successful self-employed salesman, his career was nearly over because he couldn't concentrate on his customers' needs. All his medical tests were normal, and nothing helped.

So I brought Jake to Baboquivari Peak in southern Arizona, a sacred place for the Tohono O'odham people, given to them, according to their tradition, along with the surrounding lands by the deity I'itoi or "Elder Brother." The rocky spire stands like a giant arrow pointing to God. When the sun is just right it reflects off the top, while the shadow engulfs you. The image is memorable. The hike is hot, and the sweat trickles down your back, but when the shade covers you and a light wind blows, an evaporative cooling effect can even cause a shiver that adds to the impression of being in an unusual presence.

Ever hike along a trail or up a hill, focused on staying on the trail, or on not having a branch slap you in the face, until suddenly the trees open up and you see a breathtaking valley below? In that moment you feel at one with the peak and the valley below, and a part of something grand and greater than yourself.

Deserts breed prophets

Three of the world's great faiths began in the scarcity of a similar desert in the Middle East. Stand atop the arid beacon of Baboquivari, and you'll know why deserts breed prophets. As I stopped along the way to admire the view or to sip water from my canteen, Jake chugged pills. Once astride Baboquivari Peak you can see for thirty or forty miles, even into Mexico.

"Makes you feel small," said Jake reflectively.

"How about your problems?" I asked.

"Small compared to this," he said with a hundred-mile stare.

I took a piece of igneous rock and placed it in his hands. "Put this on your desk at work."

"A paperweight?" he asked as he brushed dust from its ebony surface. A small spider hiding in one of its cracks leapt for safety on his sleeve. Jake held his arm near an outcropping and his unexpected passenger scurried away.

"No, a reminder that your problems are real, but are small if you allow them to be," I said.

Jake placed the rock on his desk next to his phone at work. When he gets irritated, he thinks of the rock, the place, and the new perspective. It helps. He recently told me that when he is cremated, he wants his ashes spread at Baboquivari Peak.

How to create a sacred place

The Plains people travel to the Black Hills, and the Hopi pray to the San Francisco Peaks, the sacred home of the Katsinam. But you don't need hiking boots, a canteen, or a compass to create your own sacred healing place.

"How big are my problems?" I ask when I look at my personal sanctuary, the sacred corner of my desk where I keep healing icons, including the pink ribbon that reminds me of a relative with breast cancer. "How should I spend my day? What if I or someone else is taken away? Shouldn't I use my time more wisely and be with them more, not less?"

What if you have a fatal illness? Should you feel sorry for yourself and hide, or get your house in order? One suggestion: Create a box of memories that reflect how you feel looking back over your life, and over the people to whom you feel close. Will it to someone as an ethical legacy of what you stood for, what you believed in.

Crisis and renewal

Hap was a successful middle-aged physician. He had a huge house, two new cars, a delightful wife, a well-paid profession, two great kids, and the general respect of the medical community. But something was empty inside him. "Is this all there is?" he asked me. "I can't imagine spending my life seeing patients every day."

"What about your writing, consulting, kids and friends?" I suggested.

Somehow it wasn't enough. Soon he was driving recklessly, seeing another woman, canceling an entire afternoon schedule at the last minute to have an afternoon tryst with his girlfriend, and on and on. His clinic staff caught on when the calls back to the girlfriend filled his day. What could anyone say to Hap?

Many Native healers have told me their personal journey to their profession was ignited by similar circumstances. The Native healing journey begins at any age, but often a crisis or middle-age itch propels a Native healer to adopt the healing arts full-time or more fully than before. Maybe this is what will happen to Hap, eventually.

Among the Iroquois, a personal illness, a personal near-death experience, or witnessing the death of another sometimes brings about the transformation to being a Native healer. Often the crisis is due to health-threatening behavior. Perhaps that is why Native healers are so skeptical about government announcements of the latest war on a disease with much-hyped new treatments, when they know from their experience and from Western medicine that most of the causes of many conditions can be traced to bad behavior.

Illness as a life journey?

Can illness be considered as a meaningful part of a life journey? Native healers view illness not so much as a force to be countered or attacked, but as a marker or a signpost on a life journey that reveals something that is not right.

Warning signs and behavioral causes

Early chest pain foretells a damaging heart attack and may be read as the body's warning to quit smoking, for example. Those who ignore these warnings suffer illness.

Consider the behavioral causes of certain cancers. Tobacco use leads to cancer of the lung, bladder, throat, and lips. Occupational exposures cause cancer of the lung, including mesothelioma from asbestos and bronchogenic cancer from uranium mining, as well as skin cancer from sun and bladder cancer from dyes. Sexual activity can cause Kaposi's sarcoma from HIV (human immune deficiency virus) and cancer of the cervix from HPV (human papilloma virus).

The cause of health-threatening behavior

Western medicine lists unhealthy behaviors: smoking, overeating, alcohol, drugs, or sex. A Native healer will tell you that these are only symptoms of a root cause. Harmful behavior is really due to conflict with others or a lack of inner peace. You've heard the expressions "smoke the peace pipe" and "bury the hatchet." Both are Native American-derived terms for the process of resolving conflicts that destroy health and harmony.

Terrorist attack in America

Imagine you're a father who has just lost your daughter in a brutal terrorist attack. The perpetrators struck without warning or reason, killing many in your hometown. After bitter tears of grief and anguish, your anger turns to what? Revenge . . . or peace? The setting is New York State. The father—Hiawatha.

"Nation shall not lift up sword against nation, neither shall they learn war anymore" (Isaiah 2:4).

(These words are inscribed on a wall at the United Nations headquarters in New York City.)

Hiawatha (c. 1450) is one of those rare figures in human history who chose an unexpected path to healing: peace. Instead of plotting destruction, he planned and skillfully crafted an enduring compact between his tribe and five others, a treaty that ended war and ensured regional harmony for the benefit of all. Weapons were buried at the base of a prominent white pine tree, and pine needles from that species (*Pinus stobus*) have been used by Native healers ever since.

Healing pines

White pine needles are actually a good source of vitamin C and when chewed also serve as a mouth freshener. If brewed, they make a refreshing tea and body wash. The Iroquois used other plant products for their medicinal properties, especially meadow rue, and the bark of trees such as the wild cherry and the willow (which contains salicin, a chemical related to aspirin). "Adirondack" is an Iroquois term for "bark eater."

The Great Peace

Iroquois history records how Hiawatha's harmony-seeking led to "peace, civil authority, righteousness, and the Great Law." Joined in a confederation, the tribes adopted the "Ritual of Condolence" to ensure that all voices were heard, and that an extremist could not sway the larger group to unwarranted destructive actions. The original confederation included five tribes; the sixth, the Tuscarora, joined in 1772. Later, the political organization developed by the Iroquois served as a model for the American Articles of Confederation.

> *"The heavens may send driving snow and bitter ice, but nature is in harmony. To find harmony man must also travel the path through storms and turmoil. And so the magic of the great peace came to the five nations and the warmth of their stronger sun gave healing light."*
>
> —Iroquois tradition

Six Nations, one sun — unity

Onondaga

Oneida

Seneca

Tuscarora

Cayuga

Mohawk

So it is in our time. The extremists of the world would have us seek revenge that brings more revenge. Hiawatha became an extremist, but only in his moderation and desire to seek peace. He spoke loudly, but only of the need to find common ground, and to bury the weapons of war.

Does lack of harmony and peace lead to poor health? Yes. In Somalia, while attempting to provide care for 60,000 refugees, I learned quickly that people were dying all around me for reasons that weren't strictly medical.

War disrupted food and water supplies, as well as agricultural development, and these disruptions led to malnutrition, gastroenteritis, and other related illnesses. In the more developed world, conflict also takes a toll on health. After the terrorist attacks of September 11, 2001, a pharmaceutical representative told me that sales of his antidepressant had soared.

How do you find peace and tranquility—on the micro level—while others work for it on the larger scene? The answer is inside us, say Native healers.

What are some practical methods of finding peace with your neighbors when everyone seems to be in conflict with another?

The Iroquois built their dwellings or longhouses in orientation with the Sacred Four Directions to serve as a daily reminder of the holy things in their life, a holiness that led to harmony. Most of us can't convince our local land use, planning, and zoning departments to reorient our houses or neighborhoods to conform to the Iroquois concept, though innovative builders are creating living arrangements that foster social interaction.

PRACTICAL SUGGESTION: When in conflict ...

If you have a conflict with another, ask yourself this question: If you had the background, experience, or education of the other, would you behave any differently? Realize that when you hold a grudge against another person, usually you only punish yourself. If you lose sleep or your stomach churns, you're the one losing your health, not the other person.

Make a list of the other person's insults or misdeeds, and another list of any positive things you gained. "He fired me, but then I started my own successful company." And so forth.

Make a ceremony to remove those hurts from your life—for example, one patient flushed her list down the commode.

Recognize that you might have played a role in the other's behavior. "When it comes to self-justification we are all geniuses," said Freud.

Lie down at night staring up at the sky. As your gaze adjusts to the darkness and you see stars whose light is millions of years old by the time it reaches you, ask yourself: "A year from now, will whatever troubles you now really matter?"

When we move on, we regain healing harmony in our life. We don't excuse, condone, or deny an offense, or put ourselves back into a relationship of abuse. We will have better health without grudges.

Honor the elderly

Native healers honor the elderly, who have kept alive the healing arts, language, and customs. This link to the past is vital for Native Peoples, especially since some have not had a written language until recently. Not long ago I met the gentleman who helped the Hopi put their ancient tongue in writing. And another Hopi elder recently invited us to his 840 moons birthday—his seventieth. The elderly are a vital link in the healing chain. In the past elders transmitted all knowledge, but now where I work, if a computer doesn't operate, the forty-seven-year-old professor asks the eighteen-year-old freshman for help. Fortunately, Native healing is centuries old, enduring, and not easily replaced by a hard drive. When we find and appreciate links to the past in our own existence, we feel connected to the larger circle of life.

Elders and healing: ways to connect

Many of us reconnect with our parents as they age and ail. The so-called "sandwich" generation is an example, made up of those who are still raising their children yet also caring for their ill parents. Perhaps these times in our lives demonstrate the Native healing principle of incorporating a community in health, whether it be help from family, the Senior Center or Meals on Wheels (meals delivered to elders).

Among Native cultures, the elderly are treated with respect as reservoirs of knowledge and sage advice. They may guide a young person on a vision quest—a journey of inner reflection and search for future direction. Rather than being a burden, the elder person is considered a treasure trove of needed guidance.

How do you connect the young and the old when you're competing with modern media, Walkman's, Nintendo, and other electronic distractions?

- Start young if you can. A ten-year-old may be more interested in a bird-watching hike with Grandfather than a seventeen-year-old.
- Make it easy. If I take my six-year-old to a museum, she is bored in ten minutes. If I have her climb up and down the steps to the place, or ride the escalator, she is engaged. Have grandparents join in

counting the steps or other activity to build connections between generations.

- Try low-tech. Kids love to show off what they have done or seen. Buy a scrapbook, glue, and markers. Have grandparent and grandchild create an album of a family gathering or trip. Let them take turns describing the photos and writing down relevant or funny comments (this also helps me, the aging parent, remember months later what the picture was about, where or why it was taken, etc.)
- Or use technology to generate generational interest. Have your child videotape the grandparent. A few interview questions will help to prime the elder's memory pump.
    - What was your first job?
    - Where did you meet grandma/grandpa?
    - What was your best memory as a child?

Adjustment to change

The most difficult aspect of making connections can be the shifting boundaries of the elder person's self-sufficiency and dependence. As the elder ages, independence declines, but not all at once or predictably. Sometimes distance hampers our ability to connect. Other relatives or caregivers may resent your involvement, though usually it is the reverse. Ask if there is one thing you can do, and offer suggestions, such as driving the elder to the doctor.

The older person may not even be aware that he or she is ill; changes and declining health or mental ability can be so gradual that they are accepted as normal. Art, a patient with advanced blockage of his coronary arteries, thought that his intolerance of ordinary activities like walking wasn't a sign of an illness, but just of "getting on in years." At first it was difficult to convince him that he was a heart attack waiting to happen. His relatives varied greatly in their response.

One daughter responded that she had been trying to get her father in for a checkup for years. Art's wife, who was in ill health and who relied on her husband for shopping and other household chores, focused on whether the pair of them could continue living independently. Another relative who lived at some distance tried to coordinate his father's health care by telephone, often at cross purposes with the local relatives who were more cognizant of Art's failing health and needs.

How to connect and stay connected?

Three words are critical. Communicate, communicate, communicate.

For the elder this means: Plan for the future. Nobody gets out of life alive. Most of us don't go from good health to death without a transition through dependency. Think through what you want if you are unable to care for yourself in stages. Talk with those you trust and write it down. Why? To avoid disparities between what one relative or caregiver heard, and what others thought they heard. And finally, obtain a living will and a durable power of attorney.

For the relatives this means: Question, question, question. Ask elders what they would have done differently when they were involved with their own parents' declining years. For example, I was troubled because my aging mother refused to get a will. "My health is okay," she countered initially. My response that every adult should have a will regardless of their health (you could be struck down by a car, etc.) went unheeded. Finally, I asked what she wished had gone differently when my grandmother was dying. After some prompting she answered, "She didn't get a will until the week before she died, can you imagine?" Unfortunately, I could. I also had to relieve any misapprehensions on her part that I was after her stuff. I told her my interest was to avoid the state taking over assets, to prevent unneeded legal hassle, and to diminish disputes among surviving relatives. I suggested she attend a seminar on dying and documents (wills, living wills, durable power of attorney).

Going into what lies beyond

Does one really live upon
the earth?
Not forever on the earth,
only for a short time here.
Even jade shatters
Even gold breaks
Even quetzal plumes tear
Not forever on the earth,
only a short time here.
—Nahuatl (Aztec) poet

"This one is ready to speak." said the Tohono O'odham healer who walked with us a few years ago among the graves of his people. He touched his long, gnarled walking stick, which looked like a thin dark muscled arm, against another grave. "This one isn't ready."

Native healers see "the beyond," and what we call death, as a transition to the next world. One such healer described the "taking up" of the dead by departed family members:

"Suddenly the light changes over the dead person," he said. "A whirling mass of roundish lights appears, leaving a dark trail behind it, all in an area of four to five feet in diameter, unlike anything you've ever seen before. It is not like what you see when electrical lights in the room change, flicker, or dim."

He continued: "The entire room fills with something—energy. At the same time this something concentrates near the head of the dead person.

"Then," he said, "you feel that the 'somethings' within this whirling mass of lights have personality. They might be ticked-off, angry—maybe at me or the family or the situation of death delayed unnecessarily by futile medical intervention? The source of this feeling has a name, sometimes of a departed relative. Others are there, perhaps many."

He paused, and then he went on: "They gather up something from the dead person, their soul, spirit, consciousness ... a light seems to remove itself from the dead person, and then everything appears to vanish from the room."

Along with this movement, according to the healer, comes a sound of energy and a fluttering like feathers. Listening to him I thought I now knew why the ancients believed angels had wings, but the healer said this was more like a mechanical sound, which ancient people may never have heard. In our time, power sounds are common.

"The light changes over the dead, becomes less illuminated," the healer said. "The dead one is finally and fully gone."

Death—the next world

In his vision, the dead are gathered up by those who knew them. What Native healers like him convey to others is a hopeful promise of eternal togetherness with those you love!

Others describe the healing light. Remember Joe, the Yakima healer who turned the corner into the light during healing ceremonies? His ceremony reaches into something greater than the self—where the soul lives—where Native healers believe all of us go. Native healers see the energy from distant stars and believe their people when they die become like a star, forever shining brightly in the heavens.

What about the rest of us? We don't have "a burning bush in our backyard," as a friend of mine put it, referring to the verbal message from God to Moses in Exodus (3:2-4). To elevate your mind to a higher purpose, try writing your own obituary (see Chapter 5) or an "ethical" will, including a list of things to do before you die, what you stand for, what you are proudest of, what you would change. This is a compelling exercise if you have ever done it, even while healthy.

Healers and harmony

Life is not a race; it is an orchestra. We are connected to all, and we are eternally connected. At a death the Native healer sees and feels the lights of the deceased family members who come to collect the spirit and energy of their dead.

"How remarkable," commented one of my colleagues. "Death is like a birth into another world or existence—the spirit lives on. It occurs to me that childbirth for the fetus must feel like a death also, moving from one existence to another. From the warm protective environment, through the pain of being squeezed through the birth canal, into the harsh light and cold of the outside world." So death is for the Native healer, merely a change, a celebration just like a birth.

Modern science still does not have a physical explanation for consciousness, but near-death experience (NDE) research offers a compelling preview of the next world. Science suggests a validation of folklore. NDE studies reveal a surprising consistency of recollections of individuals who have nearly died and been resuscitated. Common responses of survivors include a sense of traveling through a tunnel towards a light, and a feeling being outside their bodies and seeing the medical team conducting their rescue. (The work of Newberg and D'Aquili with SPECT scans, as previously described, also suggests that a higher reality exists, by showing blood flow to the orientation area of the brain during meditation.)

Native healing reaches into the soul, the inner harmony of us all. "What's the secret of Native healing?" someone asked me. The answer is, "Inside you." You are part of the whole, which includes all who have preceded you, and together you are far greater than the sum of the parts, and because of that, your healing capacity is manyfold.

There is an old story of a seeker who asks a wise man for the meaning of life. In response the sage gives him a coat with two pockets. In one is a message that says, "The Universe has millions of stars, and you are but a grain of sand." In the other pocket, the message says, "The Universe was created just for you."

Resources

Bertelli AD. Preconquest Peruvian neurosurgeons: a study of Inca and pre-Columbian trephination and the art of medicine in ancient Peru. Neurosurgery. 2001;49(2):477-8.

Brinton DG. Ancient Nahuatl poetry. New York: AMS Press;1991.

Gade DW. Inca and colonial settlement, coca cultivation and endemic disease in the tropical forest. J Hist Geor. 1979;5:263-80.

Greyson B. Dissociation in people who have near-death experiences: out of bodies or out of their minds? Lancet. 2000;2;355(9202):460-3.

_________. The near-death experience scale. Construction, reliability, and validity. J Nerv Ment Dis. 1983;171(6):369-75.

_________. The psychodynamics of near-death experiences. J Nerv Ment Dis. 1983; 171(6):376-81. Review.

Kelly EW. Near-death experiences with reports of meeting deceased people. Death Stud. 2001;25(3):229-49.

Lester D. Major dimensions of near-death. Psychol Rep. 2000;87(3 Pt 1):835-6.

Orne RM. The meaning of survival: the early aftermath of a near-death experience. Res Nurs Health. 1995;18:239-47.

Silverblatt L. The evolution of witchcraft and the meaning of healing in colonial Andean society. Cult Med Psychiatry. 1983;7(4):413-27.

Simpson, SM. Near-death experience: A concept analysis as applied to nursing. J Adv Nurse. 2001;36:520-6.

14

Your New Beginning

I am whole I am healthy I am not the disease,
I am part of the eternal greatness.
May this story give you strength. You have everything you need.
Look North: the spirit runs through the body.
Look East and feel the power of the Wind, our family, our people.
Look West and hold on to a healing guide.
Look South and make harmony with your life.

Dreaming of Heaven

Native healers hum or sing healing words to refocus us from disease to health, from pessimism to optimism. The journalist Norman Cousins helped to heal himself from life-threatening disease with laughter. "I always read the comics first," said another astute person. "It puts me in the right frame of mind for the news."

During the troublesome moments of life, when we are ill or in disharmony, we may even feel like the disfigured main character in Andrew Lloyd Webber's musical drama *The Phantom of the Opera*. Singer Michael Crawford described his leading role as that of a tragic character, "a lamentable gargoyle burning in Hell but dreaming of Heaven." Fortunately, even during the darkest days we are never alone. An inner healing potential is always with us. So important is this comforting message that Native healers add prayer to their healing to remind us of our eternal connection.

I discovered this inseparable togetherness a few years ago on a three-day backpacking trip to the bottom of the Grand Canyon, my own vision quest. The first day I was so engrossed in counting blisters and massaging sore muscles that I forgot why I came—to witness this most beautiful place where Nature took the continent for a canvas and used the Colorado River as a brush.

But, it is, after all, only rocks and water. The learned geologist will expound on the Grand Canyon's various layers. The sober hydrologist will decipher the area's watershed and seasonal flows. The observant engineer will interpret the mining efforts of early prospectors.

Yet there is more to the Canyon than this; its arches and reefs of living rock are the testament of journeys begun, a scrapbook of our species. The Colorado River overflowed when Florence Nightingale founded modern nursing in the misery of the Crimean War. Its molecules chiseled boulders when Pharaoh's Jewish slaves made bricks. Its roaring mist boomed when man's ancestors climbed into the tops of trees to escape roaming tigers, blinked back fear, saw stars for the first time, and wondered. Each stone in this canyon represents a scripture in the book of getting started with enthusiasm (from the Greek *enthousiasmos, en + theos* = "in God") on a healing journey of harmony.

Few are those who see with their own eyes and feel with their own hearts.

— Albert Einstein
(1879-1955)

A healing of higher purpose

That evening, while I was lying in my sleeping bag at the bottom of the canyon, the immensity of this creation reached inside me. There I was in the deepest furrow of the hand of God, where rocky spires enveloped me like fingers. Surely I too was part of this Grand Canyon, a piece of all great journeys, a portion of these droplets of moisture cobbled together to form a river, crashing on rocks, creating breathtaking canyons, sometimes shivering on the bank, deciding whether to plunge. Even the cells in my body were miniature mirrors of the canyon, each one the culmination of a billion years of tumultuous mutating serendipity, every strand of my DNA ready to unravel and weld with that a fellow traveler to create another human being.

It is easy to feel small in a place like the Grand Canyon, like some unimportant speck of dust on a park ranger's jacket. But like the water molecule that carves a canyon and the white blood cell that saves a human life from disease, this place is a reminder that each one of us is holding an open invitation to something grand, an adventure of higher purpose: to discover our own healing potential, to learn CPR and save a life, to raise a child and ensure the future, to donate food to hold back hunger, and on, and on. All it takes is the courage to hold one's breath and jump in. As the poet Christopher Logue wrote:

Come to the edge.
It's too high.
Come to the edge.
We might fall.
Come to the edge.
And we came
And he pushed us
And we flew!

Our great leap

A summary of what we covered in the four sacred paths to health.

North: the spirit runs through the body — spirituality and healing (wak'a)

The sacred way of life or wak'a guides Native healers. Wak's has no equivalent in our vocabulary. Sacredness, stewardship of our bodies and Nature's bounty, and self-esteem are all inadequate. Native healers do not separate the body from the mind or soul. They:

- Heal a broken spirit
- Create a vision of well-being
- Find and remedy the true cause of illness

Recall the cases of Beth and Harold: Neither could relax, and their bodies were suffering until they learned how to use reflection, guided imagery, and relaxation techniques.

East: the power of relationships — healing as a group activity

In contrast to practitioners of alternative and Western medicine who often limit their health advice to individuals, Native healers explore and promote the powerful effects of family and community on personal health, including:

- Healing and connecting with community and family
- The importance of ceremony

Sky and Larisse were reconnected with their family and community through the methods of the talking circle, table talk, and Recovery Together.

West: restoring healing balance — Native healers

Native healers do not see individuals as solitary patients who are objects or recipients, but rather as health "partners" who, with their community, participate as resources in their recovery.

Healers may:

- Promote the ill person's purification
- Develop the healing person's living in a connected world.

Through sweat lodge and other ceremonies my attending physician, Old Man Hosteen, Jack, Jackie, and Rachel restored their balance and health.

- Choose widely and wisely from Native and Western medicine.

Celestina endured the dark side of a healer. (Preventive strategies may help.) Aaron's healer saved his life.

South: the healing life cycle

For Native healers wellness is restored when mind, body, spirit, and community are in harmony within a natural cycle that encompasses:

- Childbirth and beginnings
- Grief and endings
- Blessings, sings, chants, and cures
- Space and place in health (hozho)

After a painful divorce, Jake was able to recover his sense of well-being by developing a sacred place.

Books must end, as this one does now. But the Inuit and other tribes never say goodbye. Those who part company in these cultures know they will see one another again, either in this world or the next. So it is with Native healing. There are no farewells, only best wishes on the journey to health. Travel well. Be well.

A Native healer's prescription for health

Rx: Take small miracles daily:

For a second, let it stop: the rush, the deadline, the self-imposed slavery of "must do."

For a moment, close your eyes in the darkness and see the dancing stars behind your eyelids.

For a minute, see a magnificent flower in your mind; add the sound of a soothing waterfall, and then the smell of cool mint.

For a time, feel each breath. With each breath, breathe out and imagine releasing a pain, an ache, a worry. With each breath in, absorb a sense of comfort, a kind word, a selfless act, a memory of the best thing this year.

For a life, remember:

- *North. In the spring the corn tassel blossoms with new life.*
- *East. In the summer the flower partners with the bee to fertilize and yield fruit.*
- *West. In the fall the people harvest the fruit to sustain life.*
- *South. In the winter the mountains grow white beards, and the people store food and seed to begin again, and again, and again.*

Find peace, health, wholeness, connection, and completion in the small miracles.

Healing Words: Glossary of Native American Terms

Diné (DEE-nay, "the people"). Native American nation located in Arizona, New Mexico, and Utah, also known as the Navajo. **Dinetah** means the Navajo or Diné homeland, which is approximately the same size as Maine.

Hopi (HOPE-ee, "the peaceful people"). Native American Pueblo dwellers of northern Arizona. Their ancient Katsinam ceremonies are in many cases healing rites.

Hozho (HO-zo, from Navajo). A complex Navajo philosophical, religious, and aesthetic concept roughly translated as "beauty." Hozho also means seeking and incorporating aesthetic qualities into life; it means inner peace and harmony; and it means making the most of all that surrounds us. It refers to a positive, beautiful, harmonious, happy environment that must be constantly created by thought and deed. Hozho encourages us to go in beauty, and to enjoy the gifts of life and nature and health.

Katsina or **kachina** (kat-SEE-nah, ka-CHEE-nah), singular; **katsinam**, plural (from Hopi). The katsinam are the spiritual guides of the Hopi people. By tradition they dwell in the sacred San Francisco Peaks of northern Arizona and visit the Hopi mesas during the growing season. They convey the personal prayers of the Hopi to their gods. Katsina carvings are made by the Hopi and used as a teaching tool for children, who are initiated into their religion between the ages of eight and twelve. Katsinam are also represented in ceremonies by masked dancers.

Tohono O'odham (toe-HONE-oh-AH-tum, "the desert people"). Native American nation, formerly known as the Papago, who live in the Sonoran Desert of southwestern Arizona and northern Mexico.

Quechua (KETCH-wa, from Spanish, "plunderer"). Native American language family with about thirteen million speakers of many dialects in Andean areas of Peru, Ecuador, southern Colombia, Venezuela, northern Chile, Argentina, and Bolivia. Quechua was the language of the Inca empire.

Wak'a (WAH-kah, from Quechua). An Inca word meaning sacredness, including the sacred connection between body and spirit, individual and cosmos. Sometimes spelled "huaca,""guaca," or "juaca" in Spanish, the term also refers to ancient deities, pre-Columbian artifacts, sacred shrines and archaeological sites (particularly ceremonial pyramids or temples), places underground, and hidden treasure.

Yei (Yay, from Navajo). Holy ones or gods to who lead the ill to health and wholeness, and who provide guidance for the Navajo. Their images are depicted in sand paintings. Yei'Beichii is the grandfather of the Navajo gods.

Yoeme (yo-EH-meh, "the people"). Native American nation of northern Mexico and southern Arizona, also known as the Yaqui.

Selected Reading

General reading on Native healing

Atwood MD. Spirit herbs: Native American healing. New York: Sterling Publishing Co.;1998.

Davies W. Healing ways: Navajo health care in the twentieth century. Albuquerque (NM): University of New Mexico Press;2001.

Kavasch EB, Baar K.American Indian healing arts: herbs, rituals, & remedies for every season of life. New York: Bantam Doubleday Dell Books;1999.

Lyon WS. Encyclopedia of Native American healing. New York: Norton;1998.

Mehmet O. Healing from the heart: a leading heart surgeon explores the power of complementary medicine. New York: Dutton;1998.

Mehl-Madrona, L. Coyote medicine: lessons from Native American healing. New York: Simon and Schuster;1998.

Botanical remedies

Duke JA. The green pharmacy herbal handbook. New York: St. Martin's Press;2002.

Foster S. A field guide to western medicinal plants and herbs. New York: Houghton Mifflin;2002.

_______. The herbal drugstore. New York: Barnes & Noble Digital;2002

_______. Herbs for your health. Loveland (CO): Interweave Press;1996.

Graedon J, Graedon T. Dangerous drug interactions. New York: St. Martin's Press;1999.

_________________. The people's pharmacy. Rev. ed. New York: St. Martin's Press;1997.

Johnson L. Pocket guide to herbal remedies. Malden (MA): Blackwell Science;2002.

McGuffin M et al., editors. American Herbal Products Association botanical safety handbook. Boca Raton (FL): CRC Press;1997.

Pizzorno J, Murray M. Encyclopedia of natural medicine. Roseville (CA): Prima Publishing;1998.

General reading on topics related to Native healing

D'Aquili E, Newberg AB. The mystical mind: probing the biology of religous experience. Minneapolis (MN): Fortress Press;1999.

Kubzansky LD, Sparrow D, Vokonas P, Kawachi L. Is the glass half emply or half full? A prospective study of optimism and coronary heart disease in the normative aging study. Psychosom Med. 2001;63:910-6.

McGinnis JM, Foege WH. The actual causes of death in the United States. JAMA 1993; 270:2207-12.

Murray J. Surgery of the soul: reflections on a curious career. Canton (MA): Science History Publications;2001.

Weil, AT. Health and healing. New York: Houghton Mifflin;1995.

Index

N

O

P

Q

R

S

About the Author

W.F. Peate has lived and worked with Native Peoples and healers in Africa, Latin America, and the reservations and barrios of the United States. Of Mohawk-Onondaga and European-American heritage, Dr. Peate is a native of the American Southwest. He received his medical degree from Dartmouth, followed by a master's degree in public health from Harvard. He is a physician and professor of medicine and public health at the University of Arizona, where he is a colleague of Dr. Andrew Weil. His writing has appeared in Newsweek, and his previous books include *On the Serendipity Road, Cold Peace, Genome 2,* and *Ergonomics: A Risk Manager's Guide* (with K.A. Lunda). Dr. Peate lives near Tucson, Arizona with his wife, who is also a physician, and their three daughters.